Mother Earth is Calling You

WINTER WISDOM
by Sonraya Grace

ISBN:

978-1-913590-77-2 (Paperback)
978-1-913590-78-9 (ebook)

Cover design by Lynda Mangoro.
Illustrations by Louise Coralie Hampden
Poetry by Sonraya Grace
Copy editor Anna Bromley

The Unbound Press
www.theunboundpress.com

Hey unbound one!

Welcome to this magical book brought to you by The Unbound Press.

At The Unbound Press, we believe that when women write freely from the fullest expression of who they are, it can't help but activate a feeling of deep connection and transformation in others. When we come together, we become more and we're changing the world, one book at a time!

This book has been carefully crafted by both the author and publisher with the intention of inspiring you to move ever more deeply into who you truly are.

We hope that this book helps you to connect with your Unbound Self and that you feel called to pass it on to others who want to live a more fully expressed life.

With much love,

Nicola Humber

Founder of The Unbound Press
www.theunboundpress.com

Praise for Mother Earth is Calling You - Winter Wisdom

Monica Kenton, Spiritual Guide, Shamanic Dream Teacher

Reading Sonraya Grace's words is like a balm for the soul. I instantly felt comforted, nourished, and supported with the words she channelled as well as the wisdom shared. In these times we live in, the need for a return to the Feminine ways is so needed. This book has many spiritual practices to help us feel connected and grounded in an oftentimes chaotic world. She is one who has lived and walks her talk. Her gentle yet powerful approach will appeal to those seeking to connect with their Divine gifts and be the change they seek to see in the world. Her ability to invoke deep Earth wisdom and activate new paths for readers is palpable. You will leave transformed after reading and engaging with the practices. I highly recommend this book.

Tanya Blackiston, Mother, Astrologer

Mother Earth is Calling You is a beautiful testament to the inner journey that we are all intuitively urged to take to return to our core and fulfil that which we have been born to be and become in this lifetime. Sonraya's words have provided me with an enormous amount of food for thought for my heart and soul -- all presented within an atmosphere of safe space that makes me feel maternally held and loved. Filled to brimming with nuggets of wisdom, practical exercises, journalling prompts and seasonal rites of passage, this book is the holistic spiritual and practical toolbox that will bring you back to yourself in a wholesome and profound way.

Sally Tyler, Practitioner of Ki Body Wisdom and Teacher

Once I picked up Sonraya's book, I couldn't put it down! My whole body resonated to the calling of Sonraya and Mother Earth's words, to become "the midwives of our New Earth," the new consciousness we are awakening to and that we are birthing together. Sonraya, gives clear and concise help and guidelines on how to start your journey of inner knowing and how you can reclaim your inner midwife, on our evolutionary journey.

Sonraya offers her own journey and those of her clients as antidotes and pearls of wisdom to assist you on your journey to finding your authentic self. There are journal questions to help you delve deeper into your inner knowing.
This book is for anyone to read and whichever gender, it will appeal to young and old. It certainly has helped me to be more connected to the rhythm of our Earth.

Nicola Humber, Founder of The Unbound Press
I didn't know it, but *Mother Earth is Calling You: Winter Wisdom* is the book I've been waiting for! For so long, I resisted the call of Winter; even though I'm a December baby. I felt much more comfortable with the yang Spring/Summer energy. But something began to unwind as I read Sonraya's words. I became intrigued by the different practices, rituals, and ceremonies she talks about. Could I actually be looking forward to Winter?

As a woman who's moving towards Crone-dom, the Winter of my own life, this book feels like a guide for this next season. And for younger women, what a gift to be able to embrace and celebrate every aspect of both Mother Earth's and their own personal cycles. Thank you so much Sonraya for writing this magical book.

Tara Reeves, Sound Practitioner and Qigong Teacher
Sonraya has written the book that I wish I could have read ten years ago when I was learning about myself and my connection to the Divine Feminine. This book is for anyone who is interested in working with Mother Earth, with their cycle, who wants to make changes in their life and who is looking for something to support them with the inner work that they are already doing.

It informs about life's cycles and the womb and then sets you up to explore how you connect to yourself. Sonraya looks at why it's important to connect with your womb and the womb of Mother Earth and how you can do that. Sonraya also weaves in why there is a need for us to do this work now and why it is important for the Earth – the contemporary connection which is relevant to everyone at this time.

This work goes further than informing the reader, it's like having someone to guide you to explore what works for you through the meditations, questions, and ideas for how to nourish yourself and engage with self-care. It's simply a beautiful book.

Sophia Schorr-Kon,
Artists and Founder of The Modern Erotic
Sarah Sonraya Grace's feminine wisdom is deeply intuitive and in tune with the rhythms of the Earth. Her heart at the front of all she creates and her openness to her elemental and creative nature is a gift to the times we are in.

Emma Robinson, Mother, Poet
Reading *Mother Earth is Calling You* felt like a gentle but insistent invitation, pulling me deep back into alignment with myself and giving me the keys to unlocking the Divine Feminine power that has always been within. It allowed the many ideas,

values and desires that have been floating within me to crystallise into a cohesive blueprint for living a fulfilled and connected life. Bravo Sonraya!

Anna Bromley, Shamanic Healer, Teacher and Author of *A Wild Adventure on the Big C: Natural Healing for Cancer with Guidance from My Dreams and Journeys*
Sonraya's beautiful book, *Mother Earth is Calling You: Winter Wisdom*, is a treasure trove of women's wisdom and practices to work with the energy of Winter. She helps us to see how taking time to work with our natural cycles – to rest and dream, to plant seeds that will sprout in the Spring – is so essential to a grounded and productive life, in tune with our own Soul.

One of the most beautiful and beneficial practices is her gentle exercise to connect with and heal our womb space. Tuning in to that unique voice of our own inner wisdom is so needed in this time of confusion and censorship. When it is hard to discern what is 'truth' in the noisy outer world, we need to listen even more carefully to our truth within. Thank you, Sonraya, for bringing forward this simple but powerful practice.

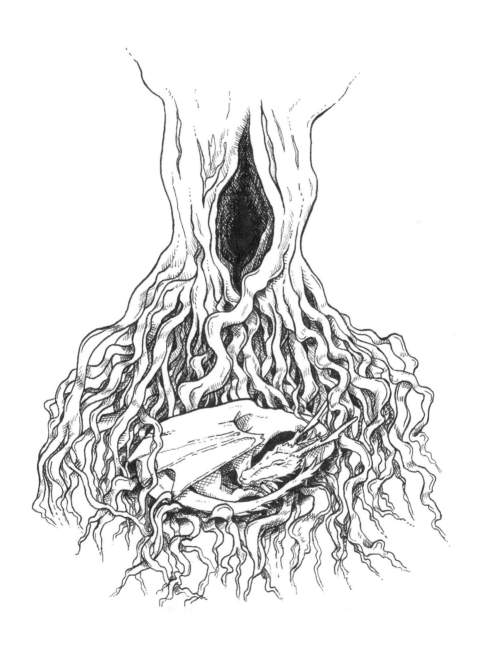

Dedication & Sacred Prayer

I dedicate this book to
Mother Earth, Gaia, Pachamama
For ALL Her love, beauty, and the bounty that she so generously gives us. Her
body is our home.

I dedicate this book to
The return of the Divine Feminine in all of us.
May we liberate her spirit, bring Her softness, compassion, and powerful wisdom
to bear, so that we may live in unity, balance, and peace.

I dedicate this book to our Ancestors and Elders.
Especially to my Mother, Sylvia Irene Dann and to my Father, Christopher William
Dann
And all those that have walked before us.
May all beings know freedom and live in peace.

Contents

Foreword

I first met Sonraya through the award-winning children's author, Hannah Gold, and her online writing group, the *Soul Writer's Sanctuary*. In reading Sonraya's words and hearing her speak, I was drawn to her warm and caring nature. Here was a woman who had made time to reflect, replenish and go within – the perfect person to empower others to do the same.

When this beautiful group came to an end, I made the decision to step up and support heart-centred writers myself, starting *Writing Inside Out* and *The Creative Writer's Cabin*.

And so began a beautiful symbiotic relationship, as whilst I might have been the coach – Sonraya was very much the teacher. And the more I read of her amazing book, the more I felt as if her words were speaking directly to me. Helping me to trust my intuition and understand better the wild and natural energies within my own life.

Mother Earth is Calling You is an inspirational book which calls to this wildness within us all. Drawing on Sonraya's profound healing wisdom, it touches a visceral chord deep within. One which has shown me that feminine energy is something to be embraced, when in the past it may have remained hidden.

At this time of immense global change, we have choices available to us that have never been possible before – yet how often do we make time to come back to this true wild nature?

I see it in the walkers I guide on England's Coast to Coast and in the many years I've spent working with people outdoors. Simply pausing in a woodland or standing on a windswept hill, awakens within us a wild magic; where once hurried or withdrawn, we can slow down and expand our hearts and minds.

Just like a physical journey, the metaphorical journey of life has bumps and issues along the way. When love and understanding are needed more than ever, Sonraya gently challenges us to embrace a more feminine approach. She shows us that it's okay to spiral in and out, that we can allow, rather than force, that we can become more patient within our own lives and be far richer for it.

Whilst it may not always be easy, this celebration of our wild, divine selves, becomes a more meaningful way of life, the more we embrace it. And through a nurturing, wise-woman style, Sonraya weaves uplifting poems, anecdotes, observations, and life lessons, to help us connect more deeply to ourselves and the world around us.

Thought provoking journal prompts offer plenty of opportunity for self-enquiry; and, through her dedication to the Sacred Feminine, Sonraya gently reveals her own magical connection to the planet we call home.

I am honoured to have been entrusted with earlier drafts and so incredibly grateful to have had my own heart and mind lovingly opened to the feminine and masculine energies inside us all.

Take your time to delve into these pages, and be prepared for a gentle transformation, as you are swept along in the *Winter Wisdom* of *Mother Earth is Calling You*. For she is a book you can dip into or read from cover to cover, and always find something new.

Simply trust that you are exactly where you are meant to be.

With Much Love and Gratitude

Jo xx

Jo Roberts - Founder of *Writing Inside Out* and *The Creative Writer's Cabin*
www.writinginsideout.co.uk

Preface

"Let me hold you Dear One, as you enter a new phase of your Life.

Surrender to my touch, my love, and know you are never alone.

I am in every rock, stone, tree, plant, river, stream, and wide ocean, in every animal, mammal, insect and bird. I am within you too, stirring, awakening rising to be seen, to be heard once more.

What does it feel like to know you are Me and I am you?

Do you feel me in your bones and blood?

I am Life and Creation.

I am also Death but not that you must be afraid of my darkness.

For Light is born from my dark fertile womb, full of rich and infinite potential.

Know there are times when the old must be shed, as your beauty is ready to evolve and be reborn. I let go of my load and all that I have created in autumn, ready to go within. I surrender to the beauty of dying for it's as natural as the rising sun. Resting allows me to create and dream of even greater magnificence, fuelling the beauty for all Life to rise in Glory.

I am on a mission to ascend and evolve and so I offer you this opportunity to join me.

Surrender to my darkness, let me hold you tenderly as you shed your own skin.

Like a newborn babe, you become the pure innocence of a new Dawn.

We rise together and create a glorious New Earth.

Paradise is not just for heaven above; but for heaven on Earth, it is for us All.

Will you come with me?

Will you answer my call?

You will find me deep inside your heart and in the depths of your being.

Your Mother always.

You, my dearest child, always.

Come enter my Cauldron.

Come now rest with me."

Speaking the Voice of Mother Earth through Sonraya Grace. 20/7/22

Back in 2010, I received the first nudges from the Universe that I needed to write a book, not just any book but one that shared the voice and wisdom of the Earth. I was told there would come a time when her words would be much needed as a wave of enormous change would travel across the planet. This would shake up and shake lose all the old structures of the old ways. At the time, I didn't comprehend the full meaning and significance of what was spoken. It was a felt sense, a strong knowing that change was coming, and I needed to take my place within the overall Divine plan to help this shift in consciousness. Close friends would gently remind me and suggest I put my wisdom and ritual offerings in the book.

In December 2010, my husband and I took the journey to Poole, Dorset to explore a change of lifestyle to live close by the sea. After arriving, we rested in our hotel room. As I rose from my afternoon nap, I unexpectedly experienced a flood of words pouring through my mind like silken threads. I quickly grabbed some scrap paper and the words of my first chapter were born.

I did not realise that it would take me nearly 12 years to finish this book. But I realise now this time is perfect. Sometimes feeling it would never finish, yet always trusting and holding hope of a glorious vision of her finished. Always holding a vision of heaven on Earth and believing this was so, as if the future had already spoken.

We are experiencing a revolution of humankind and elevation of our collective consciousness that we have never experienced before. Like a snake shedding its skin, humanity is collectively and individually unravelling and shedding the old structures that are tumbling and crumbling around us and within us. If you've been feeling this pain, you are not alone, these are pains of change as the new is emerging through the death of the old.

Mother Earth is Calling You to notice the magic of Nature that is all around you, to see how she so perfectly and beautifully mirrors your own human beingness. You see, we are naturally wild and cyclical beings just like Mother Earth, but we have forgotten our natural, free, wild ways.

We do not realise that what we do to Her, we do to ourselves.

She doesn't need healing. **We** need healing and awakening from our old ways to REMEMBER our true divinity.

Mother is Calling You shares the magic and wisdom of her natural medicine so that we can choose to align and ascend with Her.

It starts by looking within. Looking into the darkness within, not to be afraid as we have been programmed to believe, but to feel the potency of our primordial feminine power that resides here.

I have written this for women because we are the midwives of our New Earth, the new consciousness we are birthing together. It is also for the men of our world that hold the Divine Feminine as well as the Divine Masculine polarity.

I'm writing from my own perspective as a CIS woman. However, it's important to me to be inclusive. My intention is that this book can be read and enjoyed by anyone who identifies as a woman and/or resonates with the idea of reconnecting with their wise, cyclical nature. When I talk about the feminine and the masculine, I am not referring to gender, but the energies that reside within all of us.

We are each called to continue to let go of our programmes and to remember the truth of our inner beauty and who we are as spiritual Divine beings having an earthly experience. We have chosen to be here to experience Earth's school of learning, and as masters of our reality we have the power to co-create paradise on Earth. Each of us carries the blueprint in our DNA of the Divine Feminine, energetic codes that have laid dormant that are now awakening. We also carry the Divine blueprint for the Divine Masculine, for we need both to fully awaken to authentically express our gifts to create peace, unity, and abundance on Earth.

Early in the writing of this book I created a ceremony with my Elders on the inner planes. Together in meditation, I connected with them heart to heart while sitting round a fire in Nature. We shared the sacred peace pipe and sang our prayers for humanity and the Earth into the rising smoke. I dedicated myself to writing this book and promised to play my part in the overall Divine plan.

Through the ebbs and flows of life's challenges, the book you hold has morphed and changed, expanded, and grown as I have grown through and with life. I have experienced those dark places of pain, where I have felt trapped and welcomed them home to my heart for healing. Although painful they have brought me great humility, wisdom, kindness and the grace to know that all happens in perfect Divine timing. As I have grown and expanded *Mother Earth is Calling You* has grown too, her voice becoming louder and clearer.

My hope is that you will feel the call of her Love, her wildness, her wisdom, and truth and feel a deep sense of belonging as she holds you through life. My hope is you will remember your own beingness, what it means to be connected, rooted, wild and free.

Are you ready to claim your wild feminine power and take the journey home with Her?

Are you ready to rise and be the leaders of our tomorrow for our next generation?

A Call to Remember

An awakening is happening
A call to remember
Our true source of power
Our alignment with Mother Earth and the Cosmos

A safe space, solid ground
She walks in Nature, She remembers her calling.
Her innate wisdom, She feels it in her bones.
It flows once again in her blood
Connected, plugged in, no longer inseparable but part of the interconnection of
Life.
She remembers
She is sensual, wild, and free
Wise Woman at heart that lives in flow with her true cyclical nature.
A blank page of the Book of Life falls open
A new chapter begins
She rewrites her own story.

She remembers her true magnificence
Born from the Great Mother's womb.
She remembers the importance of death as part of the cycle of renewal
As natural as night follows day.
She fears not her own power,
Her voice that ROARs with the wind
She remembers the deep calling of her heart
And she LISTENS
Following its guiding beat.
And even in moments of challenge, She will not shy away from the dark face of
death
Or pull away from pain.
She sits with it, knowing she has come so far there's no return.
With kindness, love, and patience she invites all the disparate parts of self

Home.
She sees the beauty in the letting go
Knowing in the void a new seed is planted and is stirring.
In the forces of creation
She is changed, She is her true wild self.

She remembers
And She helps others remember too
Creating a ripple across the pond
Until each heart is lit up and awake.
Through forgiveness, the world finds peace
Love, respect, and acceptance are our new way
And our Ancestors cheer and celebrate, dance, and sing as we become One,
Home
United in Love.

Unravelling to Remember

Unravelling the stories that kept us tame

Unravelling the judgement and shame

Setting us free to remember

The beauty of our heart and soul

The magic of Life that holds us

Returning us home to wholeness.

Winter Wisdom

Winter is our foundation

from which all is birthed and eventually blossoms.

Surrender to her magic

And

Touch the deeper realms and mysteries of your Dark

Feminine power.

PART ONE:

OUR SACRED JOURNEY HOME

Bone to Bone

Lying on the Earth
My spine infused with Earth
Mother rises to hold me,
Bone to bone
Gently, softly
Nothing to do, just Be
I listen.
Bubbling stream gurgles and tumbles over stones now smooth
Speaking words of ancient wisdom.

Deep within the bowels of her Cauldron
Unravelling stress, tension, the old ways
Allowing Her to hold me, regenerate Me
Held safe, nourished, loved, transformed.
And here I remember All
The essence of Life
Living in rhythm and flow with the seasons
I AM the interconnection with all Life.

I feel her in my bones, damp, earthy, wild
I feel her in my blood, red pulsating, flowing
Heartbeat together
She reminds me I am Her
And She is me.
Wild, free, unravelling my ecstasy
I love Her and She loves me.
Her child resting in the Garden of Eden
She calls me to my wild heart
For here is where I merge with her Magic.

Lying on the Earth
Back bone, infused as One
I open my eyes
I see through Her eyes
The Sky, the Sun, the Moon, and the Stars reaching down to touch me

Spinning gently in the Cosmos
We are One moment of stillness
Peace

Introduction

Mother Earth is a constant, powerful force of Nature in our lives, yet do we pay enough attention to her and the pulse of life beneath our feet?

She is the creator of all sacred life. From within the womb of her being she gives birth to abundant flora and fauna. She is home to millions of different species of life that co-exist in harmony and balance, providing the perfect home. This is a miracle.

She has this amazing capacity to regenerate and renew after a forest fire, and each winter she dies back in preparation to spring forth with renewed energy and life force. She is the continual cycle of death, rebirth and renewal and we have much to learn from her.

We too are cyclical beings. This is our true nature. Thousands of years ago people honoured and worshipped our great Earth Mother recognising she is the Great Creator of all life. It became part of our ancestors' daily ritual, and many indigenous cultures still live in this way today, as they recognise by aligning with her cycles and giving gratitude for what they take, everything remains in perfect harmony and rightful balance. Nothing is taken without giving back to Mother Earth in some way.

However, with the comfort of modern-day conveniences we can forget the importance of the seasons – how they offer us the ability to shed and renew in Winter offering space for replenishment and inner reflection. It is easy for us to sit comfortably in our warm homes or catch a plane to warmer climates to avoid what the winter wisdom has to offer us. Of course, there are advantages to these conveniences.

It is amazing what we have achieved through advanced technology following the industrial revolution after the World Wars, but in doing so we have become out of balance and disconnected from the Sacred Feminine. She has become shunted, ignored and judged for being too chaotic and wild. The pendulum has swung the other way. We have lost our connection with the sacredness of living in harmony with Mother Earth and her wisdom teachings and in so doing we too have forgotten our true spiritual and wild nature.

It is sad that from a young age, we are taught to think from the logical mind and remember facts and knowledge without reference to our emotions and bodily sensations as a way of navigating life. Our gut feeling and natural animal instincts that make up our intuition, have been ignored and suppressed in favour of pushing forwards to achieve a certain result that is deemed as progress and advancement in the world.

Our disconnection from Mother Earth and our bodies that are made of Earth, can lead us to feel unsafe.

We fear change, for we fear the unknown and being out of control, as our emotions are part of our changeable nature, just like Mother Earth's weather changes. We cannot control the weather; we trust that the rain clouds will eventually pass, and the sun will emerge once more.

We can and must overcome this world problem of abuse, so that we can return to balance and harmony not only for the Planet's sake but for our own quality of life and peace of mind. For we are intrinsically linked with Mother Earth just like the interconnection of all Life she has created a home for.

What we do to Her, we do to ourselves. When we learn to trust life, to trust in the wisdom of Mother Earth that holds us, we learn to trust our bodies and natural instincts and vice versa.

There is an increasing awareness of the impact of our actions and the recent Covid pandemic that began in 2020 that affected everyone in the world brought the quality of our lives and the state of the Planet into sharp focus. I believe it has and continues to be a BIG wake up call for humanity, that has offered space to pause and reflect on the meaning of life and what and who is important. Many people have begun to make different choices in favour of a greater balance between work and family. And more people are continuing to 'wake up' from their sleep. Unplugging from mass consciousness takes time, as old structures and programmes begin to crumble and fall away, both in the external world and within our own mindset and lives.

We are on a healing journey to unlearn all the past programming of control and greed, and to reclaim our wildness, to remember our sacredness that is mirrored in the beautiful landscape and abundance of Mother Earth. Learning to love, accept and trust the Sacred Feminine and our She power that exists within each of us, I believe, is how we return to unity, peace and balance on Earth.

There is an urgent call to create change now.

Mother Earth is Calling You to awaken our true wild nature, to be the masters of our own destiny, to co-create a life of joy and abundance for us all where we live in peace and harmony.

If not for ourselves, but for our future generations, we must take charge, take responsibility for the choices we make and take action to empower our self and each other to make the changes we seek.

It starts with YOU!

Mother Earth is calling YOU is calling each of us home to be nourished by her magnificent presence, to remember the wisdom of our roots and to reclaim our forgotten Sacred Feminine power and life force.

Our Earth Mother has been a powerful force and foundation in my life and now she is calling for me to share her wisdom. She welcomes us with open arms, loving us like no other mother ever could, without judgement, without conditions. In return her love and wisdom flow to us, awakening a deep remembering of who we truly are as spiritual beings walking this Earth. We are to remember our deepest calling, the true meaning of life and the part we are to play within it. As we walk this journey home to Self, we ultimately find peace and serenity.

I invite you within these pages to join me on a magical and sacred journey through the seasons and cycles of the Earth. I have dedicated this first book in the series to our journey with Winter for this is the dark fertile space where we get to heal, rest, shed the old beliefs and programmes ready to spring forth renewed and AWAKE!

I gently guide you through your inner landscape, to heal, remember and awaken your true feminine power and essence.

Together we can make a powerful difference to our own lives and the lives of our family, our children and to our beloved Mother Earth.

This is a journey that offers you:

- A guiding hand through the season and sacred Spiral of Winter, supporting you to become a midwife to your personal transformation and rebirth.

- A Womb Wisdom map to bring you into alignment with your inner seasons within your monthly cycle, bringing an awareness of your cyclical nature and how you connect with the Cosmic Womb.

- Connection with your Ancestral Lineage through ceremony to heal past trauma and to change past, present and future generations.

- To consciously connect with your Shadow to heal and accept the wholeness of you. Discovering the magical treasures and gold within the dark and Cauldron of Transformation.

29

- Inspiration on how to sow and nurture your own seeds of creation through Conscious Dreaming and the importance of the gestation process in embodying the fullness of your own flowering.

- Opportunity for self-enquiry with journal prompts, feminine self-nourishment practices, guided meditations and simple Earth rituals and ceremonies to form part of your healing medicine.

- A deeper connection with your Earth Mother reminding you how to love, receive love and nourish yourself and celebrate the abundance that is your birthright.

- A way to celebrate your unique feminine power and wisdom with ceremony for today's modern woman that brings you into right relationship with the natural rhythms and cycles of the Earth, the Moon and the Sun.

How will you benefit? You will have opportunity to develop:

- A sense of belonging and grounded certainty in this ever-changing world.

- A calm reverence and respect for all life.

- An ability to tune in and flow with your own rhythm (we are born with our own unique rhythm that is often lost or suppressed).

- Alignment with your own source of feminine power and wisdom.

- Empowerment to trust in your innate knowing and intuition that all women hold.

- A grounded and balanced presence giving you stability and security in your own being.

- Flow with the seasons and rhythms, awakening the magic and joy of celebration into your life.

- Awakening your true passion and heart's calling, giving you clarity and purpose.

- A deeper understanding of who you are as wild, wise Woman, an opportunity to transform limiting patterns and beliefs and come home through the power of Love, to your powerful radiant Self.

If you have come to hold *Mother Earth is Calling You* in your hands, I am deeply grateful that you have found your way to taking a deeper journey with the power of Mother Earth. She will guide you home to your true nature as an empowered and authentic Woman.

She will inspire you with simple exercises, ritual, and meditations to do at home or in Nature. It offers a safe sanctuary to explore who you truly are and discover where you may be blocking your path to love and abundance.

I share my personal experience and perspective of working with the wisdom of the Sacred Feminine and Mother Earth, along with other women's stories to empower and inspire you.

Mother Earth is Calling You home to her sacred landscape, to your sacred self.

Will you answer the Call? Are you ready to journey home?

My Own Calling!

My own calling came in the late 1990's when I was working in central London for an organisation as a human resources specialist. I had worked in the City for about 10 years and was seeking something more in my life, a feeling like I wanted to break free. I had moved to a new team specialising in personal training and development and this is where I experienced my first wake up call. On a team building event facilitated by two consultants with a background in NLP (Neuro-linguistic Programming), we dived into the underlying consciousness that drives our beliefs and how we relate with each other. This was the catalyst that opened Pandora's Box and with the support of the organisation I took the opportunity for 1:1 coaching that began to uncover and heal childhood grievances.

It led me on a path to explore and heal myself deeply and I loved it. I felt I was getting to know the real me but on reflection this was only the beginning. As I transformed, the way I worked and supported others changed too. After a couple of years of coaching, I began to feel there was so much more of myself that I wanted to explore. A feeling that one gets deep in your bones that you want to find the truth of who you are. I feel this question has always been held deep within me and now my inner voice was becoming louder and more insistent.

I felt pulled between my desire to serve the individual versus following the corporate rules and expectations. I knew there was magic to life that was missing inside of me. My soul was calling for more.

Then the car accident came in 1996. When driving one day with my husband down a country lane, a car suddenly crashed into the back of us. Shocked by this almighty thud up our backend our car was pushed on its side, into a nearby ditch. I sat in shock for some while trying to comprehend what had happened. I did suffer from severe whiplash that has required ongoing treatment but apart from that we were thankful that we came away unscathed.

From a higher perspective, I saw this was the Universe's way of giving me a 'push up the backside' that was to be the push I needed to firmly step on my path of healing and discovering my true self. I was being guided in a new direction – one that was to awaken my gifts of healing, something I learnt later I had done many lifetimes before as a Channel, Healer and Wise Woman. This has led me to believe that **this earthly journey is a remembrance of who we truly are**, reclaiming our lost gifts and power and embodying them here on Earth so that we may follow our true purpose and soul's calling in life.

Within a year or so of the car crash, I was hearing the inner call of the Goddess. It came first as an internal feeling of restlessness, a niggle that wouldn't go away. I was searching again for more spiritual connection, more joy and fulfilment, until my heart led me to join a two-year Goddess course that was to take me on a deeper journey to reclaim my feminine truth. The two-year course, 'Embracing the Goddess and Penetrating the Veil' was with a loving and wise teacher, Diana Summer, who I owe much gratitude to. The course helped me connect with the powerful presence of the Goddess, the Mother of All and all her aspects. I began to see through the illusions that I had absorbed through my upbringing and society's expectations of what I should be. This was the beginning of my journey to release them and dive deep to feel the Goddess power within me.

It was at this time I felt my soul's passion to dedicate myself in service to the Divine Feminine, Goddess, and was Initiated as a Priestess and then later a High Priestess of the Goddess, in so doing I gradually came back into flow and rhythm with the Earth, seeking to connect deeper with her mysteries and through my journey finding my true self and purpose.

Many things happened during this time. In November 2000, we were blessed with the birth of our daughter. During late pregnancy I was diagnosed with gestational diabetes and although it cleared immediately after birth, after nine months I started to become unwell and was admitted to hospital diagnosed with type 1 diabetes.

On a spiritual level I could see this was my opportunity to heal, and embrace my shadow that had surfaced for healing. On a human level it was indeed a shock that I needed time to adjust to. It has allowed me to rise above and see the many gifts and blessings it has brought. It has been an opportunity to heal many of the ancestral patterning and beliefs of fear and judgement, that had been passed down to heal and clear.

Through the years I have learnt and grown in self-love and acceptance. Keeping myself well and balanced has been a priority for me. Living in flow and rhythm with the Earth cycles is where I find my peace and strength. She is my rock and foundation. It is where I listen and hear the quiet murmurings of my soul and honour my inner flow. Learning to dance to the rhythm of joy and magic in Nature has allowed me to drink the sweet nectar of life deep into my heart, my Divine birthright.

Our birthright is to live in Joy.

Let us now prepare for this journey together. Remember who you truly are, recall your lost dreams, reconnect with your roots and spiritual lineage that is calling forth the rhythm of your own soul.

Why have you come to be here on Earth at this time? What is your heart calling for you?

Let us discover together the sacredness of living with Nature's cycles, and our Dark Feminine, as when we connect deeply, we understand the purpose of our being.

I am one with the Power of the Goddess. I harmonise my wisdom and love with the sacred journey of Mother Earth. My existence resonates with acceptance and hope; I am as one with the Spirit of Nature.

The Oracle of Illumination by Vicky and Philip Argyle

CHAPTER 1

Preparing for the Journey

Practical Tips for Our Journey Together

Like any journey we take in the physical world we need to prepare ourselves for the terrain we are to walk. It is the same with our journey into the sacred mysteries of the Divine Feminine and the Earth. It is important that we create a supportive framework that we can keep returning to as this offers us focus, ongoing nourishment for our healing journey and space for reflection.

Central to the framework is a physical sacred space, a place where you can come to connect with your heart, to rest, to receive, to contemplate and meditate. This allows us to dive deeper into understanding and knowing the true self so that we may become aware of the beliefs and unconscious patterns that influence our behaviour and therefore the choices we make.

With awareness comes choice, with choice comes power and the power to change.

Let us look at what this supportive framework consists of:

1. Creating your sacred space
2. Journalling
3. Meditations

1) Creating Your Sacred Space

Choose a place either within your home and/or garden that will serve as a safe, quiet space where you will not be interrupted; a space of beauty, peace, your own quiet sanctuary that you can keep returning to nurture your soul and soothe the mind.

At home you could choose a little table or bedside table in your bedroom, perhaps somewhere where the light can dance and nourish your space during the day.

You could also create a space in your garden, perhaps under a favourite tree if you have one or a corner where you can plant flowers and lay crystals and sit in contemplation to receive inspiration.

It does not have to be complicated, simple is beautiful.

Some of the objects you might like to bring to your sacred space are:

- Winter's natural foliage
- Candles
- Crystals or stones representing the element of Earth.
- Crystals that you are drawn to or if you are new to crystals start with Rose Quartz which channels unconditional love or Amethyst which gently transforms denser energy and raises your vibrations higher so is good for spiritual growth and keeping your energy clear
- Objects of personal empowerment – may be something you have collected on your travels, images and objects embodying the Goddess and feminine and Earth wisdom.

Your sacred space forms the means for celebrating the change in the seasons and we go into greater depth about 'Creating your own Ceremony' at the end of Part One. In this way we can be reminded of our intentions through Winter and each Moon cycle, such as what we are ready to let go of and what we want to attract more of into our lives.

Once you have set up your sacred space, give yourself permission to regularly visit here to spend time meditating, journalling, holding quiet contemplation and rest. You will naturally find you are drawn to this space as the more loving energy you put into the space, will naturally grow and expand, nourishing you each time you return.

Where we place our attention, energy flows.

2) Journalling

Imagine opening a beautiful new journal, one that is inspiring and gives you space to express yourself.

Journalling is:

- An active way of committing to your journey.

- A space where you can meet and connect with your authentic Self.
- A way to unload your mind and unravel jumbled thoughts.
- A new perspective and pathway through a troubling situation.
- Renewed inspiration and a way to ground your ideas.
- Expressing difficult emotions and grief.
- Letting go of frustrations and confusion.
- Gaining clarity for your goals and dreams to make them concrete.
- Expressing gratitude for the blessings in your life.

Journalling offers a place for us to dump our thoughts, pause and reflect, find a pathway through to resolving troubling situations. Our problems become unravelled so that we can begin to see more objectively, the wood from the trees.

Through my own journalling, I have gained great insights about myself, as words that are often jumbled thoughts in my mind come pouring out onto paper, so that I can clearly see the issue in hand. It allows me to ground my thoughts, worries, things that perplex me, people and situations that have triggered me, allowing me to lay them to rest, to ground them and let them go. It also becomes a useful guide for reflection and noting how far I've come. It's great for noting dreams and piecing together dream fragments to gain greater meaning. We go into *Conscious Dreaming* in Part Two.

Journalling is a place where the creative mind is set free.

Journalling is also a way to contemplate life's big questions and as you grow in experience, to channel a stream of consciousness from your Soul and wise self.

Throughout this book and at the end of each chapter, I offer suggested journal prompts for you to contemplate. You do not have to do them all – choose the ones that resonate. Bear in mind, though, some of those questions may appear difficult and you may resist answering them. These are often the questions that will take you deeper into understanding who you truly are and what may be blocking the full expression of yourself. You can easily come back when you are ready and gently explore.

Journalling Tips

If you are not familiar with journalling and have some resistance, you are not alone. Initially turning up to a blank piece of paper can be daunting. We have been taught to identify a purpose and to expect a specific result. Journalling offers the opposite, a way to let go of expectations and allow ourselves to write freely whatever comes into our minds. You can find more tips and suggestions for how to approach your journalling at the back of the book.

The first thing is to treat yourself to a new journal, one that will inspire you to keep coming back to the page to connect with yourself.

3) Meditate to Connect

Meditation is another beneficial way for us to deepen our connection with our Self, the Earth and our higher wisdom.

Meditation comes in many forms. There are suggested meditations in the following chapters that guide you to connect with your own inner magic and feminine power and wisdom.

There are also meditations available on my website under Book Resources: www. sonrayagrace.com/winter-book-resources

Some of the suggested meditations are simply focussing your attention on your breath that leads you deeper into your body wisdom. This forms part of an essential feminine embodiment practice.

The benefits of meditation are:

- To connect us to our inner sanctuary and true sense of Self.
- To lose the noise of the outside world, to relax the mind and find inner peace.
- To come back into our centre, to feel grounded and connected to Self, Earth and the Universe.
- To develop a deeper connection with our heart and womb wisdom, to nourish our inner landscape and discover our unique gifts and qualities.
- To listen to our heart's desires and tune into our body wisdom.
- To rest and replenish.
- To connect with the nourishing rhythms of Mother Earth who feeds our blood and bones and helps us develop inner strength and resilience.
- To receive wisdom and higher truths from our Higher Self, our Soul and spiritual teachers and guides.

When we connect with our breath, we come out of our head back into our body. Our body's wisdom is essentially our feminine intuition and sense of knowing that we feel. It is important therefore that we learn to listen deeply to what she is saying so that we can learn to follow her natural rhythms, bringing more ease and flow into our lives.

Listening to our body wisdom helps us reclaim our womb wisdom, the sacred container and chalice for our feminine power and potency.

Over centuries our connection to the power and worth of our womb has been lost. Our womb holds the key to our vitality, our primal life force through connection with the womb of the Earth and the Cosmic Womb. We play a vital role in the co-creation of the Universe. Later, we explore our Womb Wisdom, guiding you in how to reconnect, to heal, to bring joy and vitality back into your life.

As you deepen in your practice and through the Earth Cycles, the womb/heart connection will be your 'go-to-place' for inner guidance, nourishment and the teachings of the inner Feminine mysteries and especially the mysteries of our dark Feminine power.

The basic meditations and feminine embodiment practices I will be sharing with you in Chapter 8 *Self-nourishment* include:

- Grounding and Connecting Meditation – rooting down into our Earth Mother and connecting with your Soul Star and the Cosmos.
- Womb Breathing – connecting to your womb wisdom and creative potency (please note you can still connect to your etheric womb space if you no longer have a physical womb)
- Walking Meditation in Nature – opening to the magic and beauty of Mother Nature in Winter so that you feel aligned with her natural cycle of death, stillness, and renewal.

Links to these can be found at the back of the book under Resources and About the Author.

She power doesn't enter us from outside,
She emerges from deep within

CHAPTER 2:
Dance of the Divine Feminine and Divine Masculine

Being a Woman in Today's World

Our perception of being a woman in today's world is changing.

Through history, women have always fulfilled many different roles and responsibilities, juggling work and families to be a good mother, wife, partner, leader and carer in our communities. In keeping busy and attending to these external demands, there has been a tendency to lose sight of who we truly are.

Beyond these roles who are we?

We have been brought up to believe that achievements and tangible results are a measure of how successful we are. We no longer clearly see our true worth and value as Woman.

As a result, many of us have suffered with stress and poor health, potentially leading ultimately to burnout and dis-ease as this inner conflict is stored at a cellular level. We have forgotten the power of our intuitive wisdom to guide us, to the extent that many of us no longer know how to listen to our feminine rhythms and the song of the Earth.

Change is afoot.

Gradually within men and women, there is a sense of 'waking up' from our sleep, seeing the limitations of the choices we have made and the effect it is having on our health and wellbeing and our beloved planet. More people are seeking increased balance, harmony and more meaning and purpose to our lives. The Covid pandemic in 2020 has contributed to this increased reflection and re-prioritising of what is important to us.

This tidal wave of movement is helping to bring balance and unity to the planet once more. Where our Earth Mother has been pillaged of her natural resources, ignored and disrespected She is calling forth an evolutionary change in the way we live our lives.

Do you feel that call, that restlessness within you that seeks for a better world?

A world that is more connected, filled with compassion and love in action, where we hold respect and honour for every living creature on the Earth.

Do you feel you no longer fit the roles that you have been assigned?

Do you experience a feeling of wanting to break free, fed up with feeling stuck, stressed or undervalued?

Are you ready to dive deeper into knowing the truth of who you really are?

If you feel a big Yes to any of these questions, congratulations, you are on the verge of a powerful awakening.

Our Journey with the Great Mother

Mother Earth is the embodiment of the Sacred Feminine and so our journey follows her natural rhythms to reclaim our primal and authentic feminine power. Our womb, whether we have a physical womb or not, is the gateway to the fertile womb of the Earth and the Cosmic Womb.

*'From the Earth's fertile dark womb of creation, seeds germinate
in the life-giving warmth and light of the Sun to flower and
become the cornucopia of life's rich abundance.'*

Focussing our attention on our unique womb space and our heartfelt connection with her, we naturally become deeply connected with the Earth's majestic womb. Her core liquid light is a place of deep nourishment and is the essential life force that fuels the potency of our authentic, heartfelt feminine expression and illumination.

'Within the dark, light is born.'

Like the Universal spiral of life, the way of the feminine is cyclical in nature and as women, we are greatly influenced by the powerful waxing and waning of the Moon.

As we lean into the Earth's natural rhythm, we also journey deep to reclaim our womb wisdom thereby increasing our intuition and inner knowing and coming into alignment with the rhythmic flow of the Universe. Our connection with our womb and the womb of the world gives us the core power to manifest all that our heart desires. We *are* the co-creators of life on earth.

The Rise in the Divine Feminine

The Divine Feminine is encoded deep within each human's DNA. The awakening we are currently experiencing is the reactivation of this dormant sacred power both within men and women, for She exists within both.

It is our role as women to be the harbingers of change, to unlock our full feminine potential and wisdom so that a new feminine principle can be birthed on to the Earth. The Divine Feminine is awakening, she is stirring, she is asking each one of us to take notice and pay attention.

Old structures continue to fall away. We can see this happening globally in politics, our economy, religion and big corporations. Also within our own lives, as old fears and patterns come to the surface to be acknowledged, healed and transformed.

What has been dormant for centuries has been awoken, her power and voice now being heard. This will continue as increasingly more women like you decide to take the journey to remember and reclaim your full feminine expression.

The Dalai Lama gave a famous statement at the Vancouver Peace Summit back in September 2009, "The world will be saved by the western woman." This was and still is our wake-up call to answer the call of spirit and align with our true nature.

I recall hearing his words that resonated deeply in my heart and core. I felt a warm tingling within every cell of my body as I remembered my reason for coming to Earth at this time; to assist in the rebalancing of all life, to help bring a wave of new consciousness that would empower us to return to unity that would be the birth of our New Earth.

We each have that capacity to awaken our authentic feminine power and *rise up*, to be the difference we seek in the world. It is already happening and more of us are awakening and are still to awake.

Expressions of the Divine Feminine and the Divine Masculine

Here we explore what it means to embody the Divine Feminine and the Divine Masculine. In simple terms they represent the 'being' and 'doing' aspects of our nature. When in balance there is a natural weave and dance between the two, creating flow and harmony within.

When we come into sacred union with these two aspects within the sacred realms of our heart, a third powerful essence of the Divine Child is created, our source of joy and innocence, and Divine unconditional love that radiates out into the world.

Expressions of the Divine Feminine

What is the Divine Feminine?

The Divine Feminine expresses herself as the qualities and essence of:

Being
Caring
Compassionate
Passionate
Beauty
Loving
Sensitive
Sensual
Sexual
Emotional
Kindness
Chaotic
Creative
Changeable
Intuitive
Receptive
Flow
Soft
Circular
Power
Warrioress
Yin
Sacred

Earth
Queen

Symbols of the Divine Feminine

Chalice
Womb
Heart
Cauldron
Rose
Moon
Lunar forces

*'When a woman rises
in her glory,
her radiance
becomes magnetic'*

The feminine is the creative force in the Universe. From the beginning of a seed, it is her loving and nurturing presence that allows life to unfold, helping seeds to grow strong roots and with the light and warmth of the Sun, eventually to flower and blossom. This is the essence of Mother Earth, the fertile container for all life.

We carry this feminine essence deep within us too. The seed of new life within our womb, whether a physical baby or a seed of an idea, is nurtured by our motherly qualities. She is caring, nurturing and gentle, her voice soothing and calming, her love being the foundation from which everything grows and blossoms.

Like the fierce lioness, she will do anything to protect her precious life. Here we see the Divine Feminine as the warrioress, as the embodiment of strength, courage and the willingness to speak out and stand up for what she is passionate about.

Like the Earth, the Feminine can be calm and soothing one day and the next can be wild and passionate, showing us that her changeable and cyclical nature is integral to her powerful nature. She is sensual, her mesmerising beauty alluring her lover, the Divine Masculine, just as we have read in myths and legends through the ages. This is the beautiful dance that exists between the Feminine and Masculine.

We also hold the 'wounded' feminine those parts of us that still hold on to shame, guilt, judgement that we have taken on from previous lifetimes and that have come down our female ancestral line. On our journey of self-exploration, we are invited to become more self-aware so we can begin to heal and release these old stories and the trauma that we may carry in our bodies.

When we come to deeply know our true nature and power as woman, with all the different aspects of the feminine, we find peace and acceptance with who we are and with all life.

Expressions of the Divine Masculine

What is the Divine Masculine?

We each carry the essence of the Divine Masculine for it is the combined energies of the Masculine and Feminine that create our inner Sacred Union and balanced, authentic power.

The Divine Masculine represents the qualities and essence of:

Doing
Action
Leadership
Decisiveness
Direction and Focus
Protector of the Feminine
Visionary
Clarity
Authority and Power
Discernment
Love in action
Humility
Logical
Structure
Container
Assertive
Strength
Sexual
Linear
Hunter
Sun
King

Symbols of the Divine Masculine

Sword
Arrow
Shield
Staff
Sun
Solar energy

*'The soul aligned Masculine
stands strong in the currents of change.
He leads with his sword of truth
with a clear vision'*

Whilst the Divine Feminine connects us with the Moon and her cycles, the Divine Masculine connects us with the solar energies, the life-giving rays of sunshine that facilitate growth and maturity.

The Masculine carries the clarity and vision and the means to get us there. He embodies the qualities of leadership, showing us the way for our Feminine to express her creations out in the world by providing form, structure, and direction.

He is protector of the Divine Feminine, cherishing her as an important ally and partner in union. As protector his *will* creates strong boundaries for the Feminine, creating a safe container that allows her to surrender to her creative flow, fending off people and energies that are distracting and harmful. This gives him purpose and when he has purpose, he can step fully into his leadership role.

He embodies strength, loyalty and carries the light of inspiration, for his energies relate to the higher mind and align with the Stars and Cosmos. He is the one that decides when it is time to act through confident assurance that the desired outcome will materialise.

He is not intimated by Feminine raw power but allows her wild ocean to strengthen his passion and sword of truth.

We can see that both the Feminine and Masculine qualities are essential for balance and wholeness within, and in all our relationships.

We also hold the 'wounded' masculine within ourselves, those parts of us still living in the old paradigm of the patriarchal society of greed, control, judgement, and abuse. The masculine also carries shame that affects his ability to be fully in his authentic power for fear of judgement. It is in the collective consciousness, so as part of our journey, we are invited to heal, release and recreate new beliefs that do not suppress our true nature but empower us and set us free.

We are also in the process of a global evolutionary shift where the active 'doing' forces of the Divine Masculine come to balance and harmonise in the heart, with the compassionate love and wisdom of the Divine Feminine.

Boundaries in Relationship

The Divine Masculine provides the safe container for the Divine Feminine to flow. The Masculine is expressed in clear and firm boundaries, in making decisions and wise choices that are in balance with both our authentic feminine and authentic masculine needs and desires.

Often, we feel overwhelmed by other people's demands, taking on their energy and being influenced by their opinions. This affects the clarity of our own energy and our ability to feel confident in our own choices and therefore safe to express what we want. As women we are naturally caring and nurturing, but we also need to ensure we are continually replenishing our reserves with self-care. This is where clear boundaries are vital for our ongoing wellbeing.

Our hips form the physical structure of our pelvic bowl and container for our womb space. The left hip and side of our body is often referred to as the Feminine expression of our selves whilst the right hip and side reflects the Masculine expression. The womb holds the combination of these qualities and is our place of central power whilst the physical hips bring forward motion, taking our creations out into the world. Interestingly, according to Chinese Medicine, the womb (known as the hara in men) is considered the second brain and power centre of our being.

What difference do you feel between the left and right side of your body, particularly focussing on your hips?

When we are in balance there is a natural dance of being and doing, like the ebb and flow of the ocean, like the in and out breath.

Become aware if you feel more dominant or comfortable expressing and operating in one way.

Become aware of any emotions that may surface as you reflect upon these. Honour these emotions with your loving attention, without judgement. Accept this is where you currently are and set the intention that you wish to explore your sense of Self on this beautiful journey with me and the Earth.

Sacred Union of the Feminine and Masculine

The aim of our spiritual evolution is to embrace all aspects of ourselves in wholeness. We are creating a new way of being, where ultimately we become the balance of both our Feminine and Masculine and celebrate the Divine Being that we are. We are less concerned with matters of the external world in which we live but focussed on living from a place of Love and inner place of union and authenticity. Here we focus on the importance of attributes and soul gifts rather than characters, roles and personalities. This is the journey to our Sacred Heart where the union of the Divine Feminine and Divine Masculine become One.

This is a journey that some of us are called to take, one that cannot be taught but experienced for it is the wisdom, love and power that returns to us through dedicated spiritual practice and soul alignment.

My own spiritual path has led me through many years and spirals of change and transformation. At the beginning of 2021, during the time of the undoing of the old structures on which we have lived, and after a period of intense spiritual initiation, I woke one night to find my heart ablaze with Light. I had been healing my wounded masculine to bring more balance and unity. In this moment I was feeling the culmination of this work on the inner planes, the unified energies of my Feminine and Masculine.

I heard the words:

'When the light of the Divine Feminine and Masculine come together in Sacred Union within our heart, the Heart Star is ignited in its full glory, magnifying, and illuminating and connecting with the Universal energies of All That Is.'

It is difficult to express the fullness of what I experienced in words other than to say my heart felt ablaze with Divine Light and I saw my connection to the stars and cosmos through my heart portal.

This experience continued for some time, and I was unable to return to sleep as the energies that were pouring in were so illuminating. The following couple of weeks I was integrating these new energies and levels of light in my physical body and energy. This was my soul light returning to me as I had cleansed and released lots of trapped trauma held in my body. I felt energy shifting in my body as the new levels of light and love settled in my physical form.

We are each on a journey to reclaim our sovereignty and for our inner Queen and King to reclaim sovereignty and sit on the Throne of our own inner kingdom. This is when the Threefold Heart Flame of Love, Wisdom and Power is balanced in the heart which becomes the magnet to attract all that we desire.

Our illuminated heart is the magnetism that draws all abundance to us.

We all have the potential to reclaim our sovereignty, our unique expression of what being in Sacred Union means. For our hearts to be the flower of Divine Light.

Our inner relationship is of course reflected in our external relationships, so the inner work is where we need to bring our attention, over and over again, to bring harmony externally. This takes time, patience, love, honest communication, and forgiveness.

We enter a new age of unity consciousness where the Earth and the Universe are creating new patterns of creation that help us move away from the struggles of the past, away from separation towards unity, to create new pathways of expansion and light for humanity. This is an exciting time as we journey back home to who we truly are and align with our authentic Self.

Journal Prompts

Divine Feminine Qualities

To what extent can you relate with any or some of these qualities of the Divine Feminine?

Write down your own expressions of the Feminine and what they mean to you in your life?

Where do you feel you may lack the expression of these qualities in your life and relationships?

Where would you like to develop or feel more feminine in your life?

What role models do you have around you that you admire? How do they embody and express some of the qualities of the Feminine?

Divine Masculine Qualities

To what extent can you relate with any or some of these qualities of the Divine Masculine?

Write down your own expressions of the Masculine and what they mean to you in your life?

What is your experience of men (as a child, teenager and as an adult)?

How many male friends do you have? What qualities and feelings do they bring out in you?

Where do you feel overly dominant in your life and what impact does that have on you and others?

Where could you benefit from more authentic masculine qualities such as strong boundaries, form, and structure?

Unity

As you reflect on your current life, do you sense any imbalance in the two qualities?

Where in your life could you have more expression of the Feminine or the Masculine?

What do you want to experience in your life? What do you want more of and less of?

Boundaries

Let us explore our relationship to the Feminine and Masculine and where we need to find balance and harmony. Boundaries between our internal world and our external world is always an interesting area that usually evokes further growth and understanding.

How empowered do you feel with regards to your boundaries, both in terms of your physical and energetic space around you and within your relationships?

Looking at each aspect of your life consider:

- With your work, clients, business partners, colleagues
- In your relationships with friends
- In your relationship with your partner (if applicable)
- In your relationship with your mother and father
- In your relationship with any brother and sisters
- In your relationship with your children, nieces and nephews (if applicable).

As you write, be aware of how you feel in your body with each person or situation.

How do they make you feel? Is there discomfort or a tension when you think of a particular person or situation or joy and pleasure?

Do you feel empowered to express what you want and need?

What changes do you wish to make with your boundaries that would feel more comfortable and aligned with who you are now?

Do you feel empowered and confident to make changes in your boundaries, to put limitations on who and what is drawing your energy?

If so, what steps can you begin to take towards this?

Note these down in your journal so you can begin to become aware of any patterns arising that are self-limiting. It is also important to celebrate those areas where you are already making progress so there is a balance with your journey.

With self-awareness comes the space for healing and making different choices.

There will be more opportunity to look at our self-limiting patterns and beliefs and how we can let go of them and transform them as we continue our journey through Winter, to awaken and embody our true feminine nature.

In the chapter on Feminine Self-Nourishment Practices, I offer an Energy Cleanse Practice and Meditation to develop Clear Boundaries.

CHAPTER 3:
The Spiral of Life

Let us first look at the bigger picture and the universal context in which we live as this informs how we perceive our lives and therefore the choices we end up making.

The world, our Universe, holds the Divine blueprint of creation within every life form. The Flower of Life is a sacred geometric symbol said to represent the Divine blueprint for creation. It is believed the shapes within the Flower of Life design represent the building blocks of life and existence and remind us of the unity of everything: we're all built from the same blueprint.

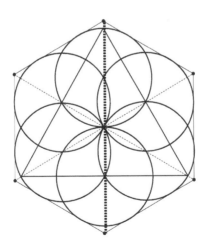

The Universe and creation is a continual cycle of contraction and expansion, of elevation and depth, of death and rebirth. Nature demonstrates this natural circular movement as experienced in her abundant life forms. Her flowers, animals and shells exhibit this beautiful flow of spiralling movement effortlessly created by the Universal energies.

If you were to trace your finger on a beautiful shell right now you will see and sense how the spiral movement of creation originates from its centre and spirals outwards in expanding circles. Likewise, if you start on the outside and trace your finger inwards you can sense the contraction of going within tighter circles until you reach the very centre.

This continual contraction and expansion happen all the time, with the seasons and rhythms of the Earth, with the tides of our oceans governed by the phases of the Moon and with our own breath, breathing in and out the same Universal life force. We are all connected in the web of life.

When we align with the forces of the Universe, we naturally come into flow and harmony with it. When we force or push against these natural rhythms and cycles and our own inner cycles, we are pushing against the whole of the Universe.

These Universal rhythms ultimately and intrinsically affect each one of us – our moods, our emotions, our perceptions, and levels of energy and therefore our level of activity.

As we deeply listen to our own internal rhythm, we are guided to either be more active and express ourselves outwards, sharing our gifts and light. On the other hand, we may feel the need to draw back within ourselves like in Winter, to rest, reflect, to heal, to nurture our inner creativity before coming out again ready to give birth to our deepest desires.

We too experience the continual cycle of death and rebirth, of contraction and expansion, within our own being. This pulse is changing all the time. It is our gift to tune in and listen carefully to our intuition and to act upon the sensations and impulses we receive from our heart and body.

How does She want to be in this moment?

Tune in and listen.

How does She feel?

Breathe and let go.

How does She want to flow with the rest of her day?

With greater awareness of our own rhythms and cycles we can begin to make better choices for our own wellbeing, health and ultimately how we choose to express ourselves and manifest our creations in the world.

SPIRAL OF LIFE

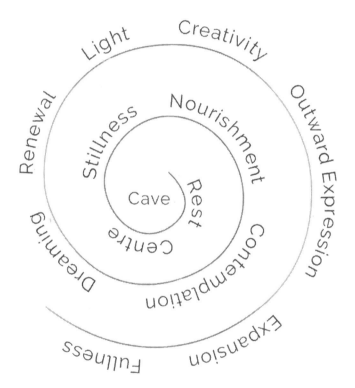

CHAPTER 4:
Wheel of the Year and Moon Cycles

Let us look at how the spiral of creation manifests as the seasons and cycles of the year, known by our Celtic ancestors as the 'Wheel of the Year.' This is based upon the changing cycles of the Sun and Moon in relation to the Earth and creates a subtle yet powerful affect in creating our seasons.

The Wheel of the Year is our map for tuning in and listening to our own inner seasons and rhythms held within the womb. This process gives meaning, depth and a grounded presence to a more spiritual life.

Rather than like our linear calendar that does not honour our natural ways, the Wheel offers an organic evolving process that supports our connection to our true cycle and natural rhythm.

This is what we must do now. Remember our true origins and take the journey back home to feel rooted with our Earth Mother and our own being.

Refer to images on next page: Wheel of the Year Diagram

As, shown in the diagram, we see the Wheel provides a circular container for the natural movement of the spiral. The seasons around the wheel begin with Winter and naturally flow into Spring, Summer and then Autumn and back round again to Winter, creating this never ending, naturally expanding and contracting cycle.

Like our ancestors, we can use this Wheel as a framework to connect with the natural Universal forces of the planet so we too can live in harmony and balance.

With conscious awareness we can allow it to facilitate a deepening of our womb power and connection with the Earth as the fertile womb of creation.

CYCLES OF THE EARTH
Living in flow with nature's seasons
Northern Hemisphere

NORTH
Winter Solstice
20-22 Dec

SAMHAIN
end Oct/beg Nov

WINTER
Death
Stillness
Renewal

IMBOLC
end Jan/beg Feb

EARTH

WEST
Autumn Equinox
20-22 Sep

AUTUMN
Harvest
Release
Cleanse

WATER

AIR

FIRE

SPRING
Awakening
Fertility

EAST
Spring Equinox
21-22 Mar

LAMMAS
end Jul/beg Aug

SUMMER
Blossoming
Abundance

BELTANE
end Apr/beg May

21-22 Jun
Summer Solstice
SOUTH

CYCLES OF THE EARTH
Living in flow with nature's seasons
Southern Hemisphere

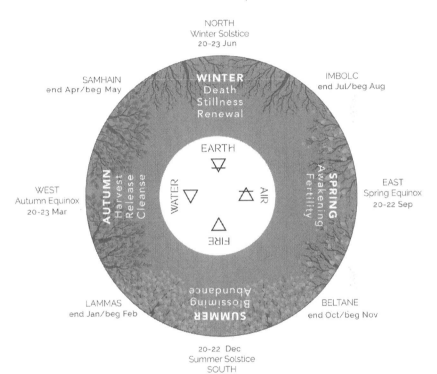

NORTH
Winter Solstice
20-23 Jun

SAMHAIN
end Apr/beg May

IMBOLC
end Jul/beg Aug

WINTER
Death
Stillness
Renewal

WEST
Autumn Equinox
20-23 Mar

EAST
Spring Equinox
20-22 Sep

EARTH

AUTUMN
Harvest
Release
Cleanse

WATER

AIR

FIRE

SPRING
Awakening
Fertility

LAMMAS
end Jan/beg Feb

SUMMER
Blossiming
Abundance

BELTANE
end Oct/beg Nov

20-22 Dec
Summer Solstice
SOUTH

The Earth Seasons and Celebrations

Equinoxes and Solstices

The Wheel is broken down in to eight points or 'turning points of the wheel', consisting of Equinoxes and Solstices further broken down into four Cross-Quarters.

The Spring and Autumn Equinoxes and the Summer and Winter Solstices form the four main quarter points of the Wheel. They create a symbol of a cross within the circle representing the ancient symbol of balance, wholeness and stability of the Earth.

In the Northern Hemisphere, the Spring and Autumn Equinoxes happen between 20-23 March and 20-23 September, signalling the first day of Spring and the beginning of Autumn's fall. These are balancing points on the Wheel and are pivotal points when day and night, light and dark, become equal.

In contrast, in the Southern Hemisphere, the Spring Equinox and first day of Spring officially begins between 20-23 September whilst the Autumn Equinox falls between 20-23 March. The specific timings in each hemisphere, vary each year depending on the alignment of the Sun in relation to the Earth.

The Winter and Summer Solstices are the peak points of our seasons and are opposite each other on the Wheel. In the Northern Hemisphere we experience mid-winter with the Winter Solstice falling between 20-22 December, whilst in the Southern Hemisphere they are experiencing the blossoming of their Summer. In the Southern Hemisphere, the Winter Solstice falls between 20-23 June, whilst in the Northern Hemisphere we are moving into the peak of our Summer Solstice between 20-23 June.

The Celtic Seasonal Festivals

The Celtic Festivals of **Imbolc, Beltain, Lammas** and **Samhain** (pronounced Sow-aine) on the Wheel form the four Cross-Quarter points. They fall approximately six weeks after the main Quarter points and signal the beginning of a new cycle and transition to the next phase.

These turnings of the wheel were celebrated and honoured by our Celtic ancestors through ceremony and ritual bringing the people into alignment with the creative forces of the Universe. It brought them sacred meaning, joy, balance, and abundance to their lives.

To this day they are celebrated, giving time out of our daily schedule, to take stock, reflect upon their influence on our feminine cycle, giving space to honour our connection with the Earth and our own true nature.

The Wheel is a powerful force for healing as we choose to consciously work with the underlying energies helping us to let go so that we can embrace a new cycle and version of ourselves, with power and intention.

On this journey we focus on the potency of Winter, as it is during this season that we have the greatest opportunity to shift and transform, to rest in the power of the dark, to heal and rejuvenate ready for Spring.

Overview of The Wheel

Winter

Themes – Death, Stillness, Renewal

Winter offers a time to slow down, to rest in stillness, to contemplate, heal and to nurture our inner world. Deep within our inner sanctuary, the seeds of new hopes and dreams are planted ready to emerge in Spring.

Spring

Themes – Awakening, Fertility

Early Spring announces a gentle stirring in the Earth, an awakening, as Nature slowly begins to wake from its slumber. Snowdrops and early crocuses prick the cold earth. Her Winter coat is slowly cast aside for new growth and fertility to begin sprouting.

Summer

Themes – Expansion, Blossoming

The peak of Spring brings an abundance of fertility with new growth being witnessed at every turn. Summer brings a period of expansion, and everything is plentiful.

Autumn

Themes – Thanksgiving, Harvest, Fall

As the exuberance of Summer begins to fade, plants and flowers that we have nurtured through the growing season are now laden with fruits and seeds offering the fullness of their beauty and nourishment to sustain us through the Autumn and Winter months.

Abundance is everywhere for us to behold.

Celebration is in the air as we reap our harvests with a grateful heart.

Let's now dive into Winter!

The Beginning of Winter – Samhain

On the 31 October, the Cross-Quarter Festival, **Samhain** marks the beginning of Winter and the descent into the darkest months of the year. This is when the energies of the old year fade and become 'thin' allowing a piercing of the veils between matter and Spirit.

The thinning of the veils at Samhain provides opportunity to connect closely with our Ancestors and Spirit Guides. We can use this phase as an opportunity to honour and celebrate those that have come before us. We can heal old traumas and patterns, offering forgiveness and creating freedom for all – not only down our lineage but energetically freeing those of our future generations whether living currently or those that are still to be born. This is exciting, as we are in a place of great opportunity for change.

At mid-Winter, we reach the shortest day and longest night usually falling on or around 21 December each year in the Northern Hemisphere. This is known as the **Winter Solstice**, a magical pause for us to sit in silence and contemplation, to appreciate what the darkness has brought us in terms of time for healing and inner reflection. At this point we celebrate the returning Light as the 'new' Sun God is birthed on our Motherland.

The heart of Winter offers a deep connection with the void and the fertile womb of creation.

From this point, the sun slowly begins to rise again, gradually increasing the length of daylight until we come to Imbolc at the beginning of February when the Earth gently begins to stir with life. From seeds that initially lay dormant in the darkness of winter, they are then released and swept up by the breeze and planted far and wide to become young seedlings. We begin to see her awakening ever so slowly from her sleeping slumber with pinpricks of light, as snowdrops miraculously push through the cold hard earth.

We experience this same fluid movement within our own menstrual cycle, our internal seasons of Winter, Spring, Summer, and Autumn that are our expressions of the continual cycle of death and rebirth. We go on to explore this in the following chapters – 'Feminine Inner Seasons and Womb Wisdom.'

From the centre of our own being, our womb space, we have the power to sow the seeds of our dreams to co-create with the powers of the Universe.

As we live in flow with the rhythms of the Earth, we discover our own way to honour and trust our inner cycles. These inner cycles become the voice of our intuitive knowing and inner wise counsel. With practice we learn to understand our own body's unique sensations and feelings and what they mean to each of us, guiding us to live in harmony with the ebb and flow of the Universe.

I have found with practice and a deepening into the wisdom of my inner cycles, I have created more ease and flow to my life, as I have learnt to trust my inner guidance, the foundation of feminine power. You too will find this with dedicated practice.

Moving through the seasons, we come full circle to become reborn at the Winter Solstice, both individually and collectively.

The Sacred Elements

Within the Wheel of the Year, you will see each season flows with the powerful elements that make up our Universe. They are the elements of Earth, Air, Fire, Water and Great Spirit.

They exist all around us and within us; in the air we breathe, in the rain that makes up our streams, rivers, oceans and glaciers, in the sun rays that give light and warmth and in the earth herself, providing a home for all life.

They weave the very fabric of life itself, including what makes up our physical and energetic form as human beings. They are constantly changing to create balance and equilibrium and the perfect conditions for decay and growth on our planet.

Understanding the magic of the elements allows us to call on their wisdom and healing power for the greater benefit of all. Living in harmony with them creates flow and ease and using them in our rituals and ceremonies adds power and balance to our lives.

During Winter, we are governed by the energy and element of **Earth** drawing our attention inwards and beneath our feet, to listen to Her calling and wisdom. She is the rocks and stones that make up the Earth, the mountains that have pushed up to create the contours of her body as well as the undulating hills that are the breasts and belly of our Great Mother. Our ancestors created stone circles and sacred sites where they could come to pay homage to the Earth and to the rising and setting of the sun at the Solstice and Equinoxes. These alignments between Earth and the Cosmos offer powerful portals to align with the star constellations to receive their light and wisdom. We explore more in the chapter *Earth's Magical Gifts* later in Part One.

This is the most common interpretation of the Wheel, although we may find that some people represent the elements in different positions. I believe we can represent them depending on what meaning they hold for us in each season, using the concept of the magical compass. Assuming our intention is clear, the energy of the elements will flow where we place them.

Moon Cycles and Phases

'The moon's silvery glow hangs low in the night sky sending shafts of beautiful light on the gentle waves of the sea. My face turns upwards to her magnificence, and I feel the connection and oneness with her deep inside my belly. My heart expands in joy as I receive her blessings. I feel reassured that I am where I am meant to be.'

Sonraya Grace

The waxing and waning cycles of the Sun and Moon offer us a framework for connecting with the energy and changing cycles of the Earth and our own Inner Seasons. The Sun provides our life-giving warmth and light that is the outward giving energy for our growth shown in the Wheel of the Year. The Sun and Moon's combined energies have a powerful effect on our planet whether we are conscious or not.

As the Moon goes around the Earth, the Earth goes around the Sun, creating a beautiful cosmic dance between them. The Moon phases are a result of the changing angles between the Earth, Moon, and Sun as this takes place.

In this chapter we explore the nature of the Moon and her influence on how we feel physically, emotionally, and spiritually and the key gifts she can give us to come into greater alignment with our feminine essence.

The following section is designed to give a brief outline of the Moon phases as she waxes and wanes and her general effect on our feminine cycle. As she is so closely associated with our feminine nature it makes sense to align with her changing cycles to help us create more flow and ease in our daily lives.

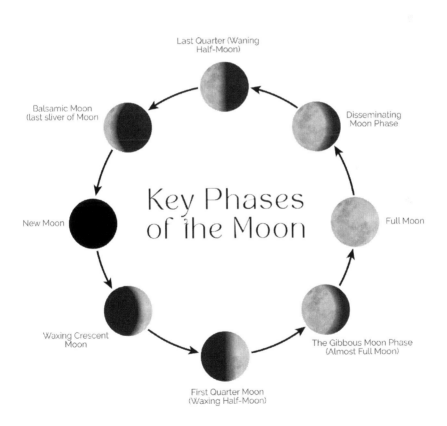

Last Quarter (Waning Half-Moon)

Balsamic Moon (last sliver of Moon)

Disseminating Moon Phase

Key Phases of the Moon

New Moon

Full Moon

Waxing Crescent Moon

The Gibbous Moon Phase (Almost Full Moon)

First Quarter Moon (Waxing Half-Moon)

There are many books dedicated to working with the Moon phases, that go into greater detail, and I have named these under *Resources* at the end of the book.

Flowing with the Cycle of Creation

Seed – Gestating – Sprouting – Growth – Flowering – Blossoming – Decay – Death – Renewal

New Moon (Dark phase of the Moon)

Key Themes:

Beginning of Spring/Maiden

Rebirth, Potential, New Promise

Active Phase: Sowing

This phase begins 1-3.5 days after the Balsamic Moon.

At the New Moon we have the Sun and Moon rising together in the East. The Sun is behind the moon so from where we are on Earth she appears invisible or dark.

This is a potent time of the Moon cycle to plant the seeds of new hopes and dreams and to welcome new beginnings. In the few days before the New Moon, we may feel a strong invitation to let go, as old energies surface to be cleared away.

In that dark void, just like fertile soil, there is space for infinite possibilities. Our aim is then to move into focussing our intentions on what we truly want, to energise our dreams and visions and to let go of anything that may get in the way of those.

The New Moon connects us strongly with the Dark Feminine and our Dark Goddess, helping us to let go and recreate a new reality. This is a potent time of the potential of what is to come with the sowing of new seeds of hope.

A New Moon Ritual

It is a good idea to set intentions in the dark fertile phase of the Moon.

Create a simple ritual lighting a candle in the dark evening.

Be ready to feel what you feel as you face the Dark Feminine and to honour her and let go of any fears that may surface. Then be ready to create a new reality; one where your heart is singing the tune of your Soul.

Write down your deepest desires or create or paint a vision map of colourful vibrancy.

Breathe and feel yourself living your best life. Call out your prayers and dreams to the Universe. Hang prayer flags of gratitude on sacred trees. Give thanks for all that is already on its way.

Waxing Crescent Moon

Key Themes:

Sprouting
Pure potentiality

Active Phase: Sprouting

This phase begins 3.5-7 days after the New Moon.

Just like the pure white snowdrops that pierce the cold earth after Winter, this is the first visible silver crescent of the Moon, seen in the western sky in late afternoon and early evening. This is the energy of Maiden, full of new promise, potential and pure innocence.

In this phase, our ideas begin to sprout in the growing presence of the Moon's light and energy. It is time for us to choose from the myriad of ideas and channel our focus to just one or two. Our new ideas start to take shape.

Journal Prompt:

What is one step I can take towards my dream and desire?

First Quarter Moon (Waxing Half-Moon)

Key Themes:

New growth
Commitment
Challenges

Active Phase: Germination

Lasts: 7-10.5 days after the New Moon

She rises at noon and sets at midnight. This is the time when the journey of the moon is moving towards her fullness. It is a time for decision and committing our energies to bringing in what we do want. It can be a challenging phase as our commitment may be tested, requiring us to overcome any obstacles, internally or externally.

Journal Prompt:

What is beginning to show itself? Congratulate yourself on what steps you have already taken.

What Universal signs am I noticing that shows my ideas and desires are on their way?

What adjustments do I need to make?

What support do I need to overcome any perceived challenges?

The Gibbous Moon Phase (Almost Full Moon)

Key Themes:

Refine
Solidity
Stamina

Lasts: 10.5-15 days after the New Moon

She rises mid-afternoon and sets just before dawn. This is an active phase, developing our new ideas, giving them shape and making them concrete. It requires tenacity and stamina to stay the course. It can be easy to give up.

Use the Moon's energy to bless your path, helping you to overcome ego tendencies. Stay open to what the Universe is guiding you to do, adapting and adjusting your plans to stay on course with your ultimate outcome. At the end of the day, we are often called to trust as we take one step at a time into the unknown. Following the guidance of our heart's wisdom is key.

Journal Prompt:

How can you pace yourself, lean into your feminine to nourish her?

We don't have to struggle and strive to complete things. Sometimes taking time out to play, to rest, brings in fresh energy, new ideas that help you sustain momentum in the long run towards completion and fruition of this cycle.

Full Moon Phase

Key Themes:

Summer/Mother
Full Moon (Expansive, Completion)
Relax, acceptance, completion
Healing and Forgiveness
Gratitude

Active Phase: Blossom/Completion

Lasts 15-18.5 days after the New Moon.

Coming to fruition of your plans, ideas, and projects. It can also represent the culmination of your inner gifts, qualities and becoming aware of limiting patterns and emotions that have surfaced during the moon cycle. They arise for resolution, forgiveness, healing, and release.

Full Moon Ritual

The Full Moon is a great time to create your ritual, to honour the phase that you have been through, to heal, let go and embrace the gifts of this cycle.

Take the time to journal and to use the energy of the Moon to heal. You can use the resources under the chapter 8 *Feminine Self-Nourishment Practices* to help you.

Set up your sacred space (see chapter 9 *Creating Sacred Space* and Sacred Ceremony for inspiration and how to honour the sacredness of ceremony).

You may like to use the power of Fire to alchemise or Water to cleanse and to let go.

Fire

You can write down what you wish to let go of and then burn it safely in a fireproof container. Bury the ashes with gratitude in the Earth. Create a fire and sing your prayers around the fire, watching it dance and burn away the old.

Water

Write down what you wish to release and let go of. Cleanse them in spring water or water collected from a river, stream, lake, or ocean. Feel everything washed away.

Swim in natural water, intending all is washed clear. A shower or bath is a beautiful alternative in Winter, if cold water swimming is not your thing.

Cleanse and Recharge Your Crystals

It is also a good time to cleanse your crystals out in the moonlight overnight, asking that they be cleansed and recharged. Use the window of the Full Moon to do this, either the evening before, the day of and day and evening afterwards when the Moon is at her peak.

Disseminating Moon Phase

Key Themes

Rest, Re-orientate, Self-Reflection

Active Phase: 3.5-7 days after Full Moon

The Moon rises mid-evening and sets mid-morning. At this Moon phase, she promotes root development and swelling of buds/fruits as she draws sap up the Earth's water table.

Last Quarter (Waning Half-Moon)

Key Themes

Autumn/Enchantress/Wild Woman
Trust, Harvest, and Assimilation

Active Phase: 7-10.5 days after Full Moon

The Moon rises at midnight and sets around noon. This phase we begin to go within to assimilate and gather all that we have been working with during the cycle, to review and decide where we want to improve. It is a time to trust your instincts as your psychic abilities and intuition are greatly heightened.

Balsamic Moon (last sliver of Moon)

Key Themes

Winter/Crone/Wise Woman
Letting go, Surrender, Forgiveness

Active Phase: 10-12 Days after Full Moon and continues until New Moon

This is the last sliver of the Moon seen in the Eastern Sky at dawn when she rises and sets early afternoon. This phase is sacred to the Crone and Wise Woman, bringing her wisdom to face the shadows, to let go of those things that do not serve us any longer, including letting go of relationships. A time to honour our inner wisdom in preparation for new beginnings under the New Moon.

How The Moon Affects Our Feminine Cycle?

Living by the cycles of the Moon, month to month, helps us get back in touch with her cycles and therefore our inner rhythms. The Moon's 29.5-day cycle corresponds with our menstrual cycle and is a powerful reminder of the ancient ways that saw women as the embodiment of the Triple Goddess of the Young Maiden, Mother and Crone (Wise Woman).

The Young Maiden, fresh with her emerging spirit, the Mother, embodiment of our mother nurturing nature, the Enchantress/Wild Woman and the Crone or Wise Woman guardian of the inner realms and wisdom gained through life's experience.

The Moon influences all the waters of the Earth, her ocean tides, streams and rivers and the underlying rivers that run deep in the Earth. All life forms that carry water such as plants, trees, animals, and mammals, are influenced by the power of the Moon, including the blood and fluids of our bodies, which make up over 70% of our physical form and female reproductive cycles. We can therefore see the Moon has great power and influence for creating change and patterns in our lives.

The Moon helps us come into our natural flow and is concerned with fluidity and therefore our emotions. There is a sense of expanding and contracting with the ebb and flow of her tides.

At the Full Moon, we may feel a sense of fullness and expansion, as her magnificence is mirrored back to us, as the Sun illuminates her. We may experience increased water retention and bloating particularly in the womb area, belly, and breasts. Our emotions may become heightened along with our sensitivities, our physic abilities and intuition.

In the opposite way, at the time of the New Moon we experience the dark side of the Moon, our true and deep raw feminine nature, as the sun is no longer shining on the Moon. Now we experience a sense of contraction and the depth of the Moon cycle as we experience a need to withdraw within to rest, let go and consult with our inner wise woman just like in the winter season. We are all unique, so honour what you feel is your experience and what is right for you.

CHAPTER 5:
Earth's Magical Gifts

The Earth herself is made up of the Element of Earth, the densest of all the elements and forms a beautiful complex structure within which all the other three elements of Air, Fire and Water are contained. The combination of them is in the form of our mountains, valleys, caves, beaches that hold our oceans, the contours of our rivers that allow water to flow, our forests, and beautiful meadows.

Earth herself is made up of the structure of rocks, stones, and the mineral kingdom. Stones are the element of Earth and are represented in our physical bodies as bones – the structure that holds our form together, keeps us upright and is the most dense and solid part of ourselves.

We can see clearly, we are Earth. Like Earth, the elements form our shape, and the marrow of our bones with its blood cell network is like the rivers and streams of the Earth, allowing essential oxygen and nutrients to feed our organs. We often have the saying, "I can feel it in my bones," and I wonder if this is our deep knowing of our connection with Mother Earth.

Stone Circles and Barrows

Our ancestors have had a long association with stones and the crystal kingdom. They would gather stones for a fire pit, would use them to bury their dead, would create medicine wheels using stones and the large standing stones, megaliths, are found in many sacred sites across the world.

Stones appear dead, lifeless, and inert; they do not move, breathe, or communicate as far as we perceive them. However, they do have a very slow vibration, and crystals have long been used by shamanic traditions and in healing work by different cultures across the world. We know that crystals can hold, record and store electromagnetic pulses, energy and therefore our intentions and thoughts, which are energy waves.

Some of the standing stones of Britain have over many years been tested by researchers such as the Dragon Project and have been shown to be exhibiting a vibrational frequency pattern described as 'singing.' The stones hold a high concentration of quartz crystal (silicon dioxide), making them large energy-conducting devices and transmitters of energy.

Tom Graves in his *Needles of Stone Revisited*, compares them to acupuncture needles in the body of the Earth, acting just like acupuncture needles that are used on our physical body to help the flow of energy along our meridians. These stones are considered to align with certain star constellations in our night sky, helping to transmit and anchor starlight into the Earth grid. This is carried around the planet via the Earth grid, allowing these starlight energies to flow and assist in elevating our collective consciousness. Fascinating.

Stonehenge and Avebury Stone Circle

Who built them and for what reason?

Archaeologists to this day still don't fully understand their purpose, considering they may have been used for ceremonies, burial, and religious purposes. The standing stones and stone circles in Britain, like the ones of Stonehenge, and Avebury Circle and The Avenue are world heritage sites in Wiltshire. Over the centuries there has been much interest in their connectedness with the stars and Gaia and how they are an essential network of interconnectedness with other sacred sites that connect with the ley lines (meridians) of the Earth also known as dragon or serpent lines. The St Michael Ley Line is said to pass through several sacred sites including Avebury, Glastonbury Tor, down through Hurler's Stone Circles on Bodmin Moor in Cornwall to St Michael's Mount at the southernmost tip. Drawing a line across these points, it travels the other way to the great Abbey of Bury St Edmund and on to Hopton on Sea. According to research published by Paul Broadhurst and Hamish Miller in their book, *The Sun and the Serpent*, the Michael and the Mary currents cross under the Obelisk in Avebury (named for their qualities of masculine and feminine flow) bringing a sense of unity and harmony. There are many books about these fascinating stone circles; Avebury by Evelyn Francis is a great little book that shares some of the fascinating secrets of this ancient site.

In the book *Serpent of Light: Beyond 2012*, Drunvalo Melchizedek explains the movement of the Earth's Kundalini and the Rise of the Female Light 1949 to 2013. He shares his journey to some of the key sacred sites around the world where he and others activated the rising of the Feminine Light to assist Gaia and the human conscious as part of our ascension process to higher consciousness. It is a fascinating read to know how everything is interconnected and plays a part in the abundance and beauty of the Earth and all kingdoms that live on her. This is a key reminder that we are all interconnected in the web of life, all humans, and all life on Earth; what we do to the Earth or to another, we do to ourselves.

Others believe stone circles were designed in such a way to align with certain celestial events occurring in the night sky. We know our Celtic ancestors celebrated the Summer and Winter Solstice in these sacred places, knowing that the sun set and rose and would perfectly align with the stones. There are numerous sacred sites across the world, where people gather in ceremony to celebrate and give gratitude for our life-giving sun.

Long Barrows

They appeared at the start of the great stone circle building period. The West Kennet Long Barrow which is a mile or so outside Avebury along the Old Ridgeway Road, is up on a small hill away from the noise of traffic. Again, people don't fully understand the purpose of these long barrows, imagining they were kingly burial chambers. Deep inside is the main chamber with small chambers leading off either side of the main passageway in. The large boulder that once closed off the Barrow has long since been moved, making it available to the public to enter.

West Kennet Long Barrow - 'Cave of Elders'

I recall taking a small group of women to West Kennet Long Barrow on one of my retreats. We really did feel we were entering the womb of the Earth – dark, damp, and silent. You could almost hear the pulse and heartbeat of Mother Earth herself if you dropped deep into your heart to listen.

In the main chamber at the end of a narrow dark tunnel, I lead our group into ceremony, lighting a small candle in the sand that we could barely make out at the bottom of the cave-like chamber. We called on our ancestors to be with us, so that we may honour the Goddess, and honour the Goddess within all women and men. We began with a song and gentle drum. As we began to drum the sound of our beat grew louder, the drum beat resonated around the walls of the inner cave. As I become one with the drum, I found I was taken over with the energy and life force that was rising through my body from the Earth. I spontaneously opened my mouth and began to chant, a chant that was not mine but coming from some ancient place.The sounds of the chant banged around the chamber loud and powerful, the primal force of ancient elders sounding their voice for all to hear.

After some while, gradually the impulse to chant abated and we became silent again, standing in the power of what we had just co-created with the ancient ones. Words could not describe how we felt. We were stunned in silence, the power palpable like you could cut with a knife. My heart thumping loud inside my chest, my legs shaking from the sheer force of the energy that had just come through me.

As we eventually came to, we gave our thanks and closed the circle.we gathered our things and made our way out of the dark chamber along the corridor. We noticed all the other tourists that had been around had left and were outside in the light of day. Our group looked into each other's eyes and faces and recognised the power within. We were changed.

Our Root Chakra

Let's talk a little bit about our Chakra system, known as wheels of energy, that feeds light into our physical body and organs, and is connected to our energetic aura that is all around us.

There are seven major chakras that are attached to the physical body that form part of our Light body, aura. They are the Root at our base, Sacral, Navel/Solar Plexus, Heart, Throat, Third Eye and Crown at the top of our head. Below the Root is our Earth Star and the Gaia Gateway and above the Crown is our Soul Star and Stellar Gateway. There are many more chakras that go above and beyond but for the purposes of this exercise we will focus just on the seven major ones.

All the chakras are interrelated and interconnected; one affects the other. When we are feeling good and our health is vibrant, we are in flow, our chakras are clear, balanced, and harmonious and so is our Light body that feeds the chakras with energy and light. If we are out of balance, our chakras will be out of balance; some may feel blocked or stuck or stagnant affecting the flow of our life force, our health and wellbeing. We can use clearing and healing techniques I share in the *Chapter 8: Feminine Self-Nourishment Practices*, or you may wish to see a professional healer who can help you clear and rebalance.

We specifically look at the Root Chakra as this is our connection to the Earth through the Earth Star.

The Root Chakra is our centre of security and rootedness with the Earth. When **in balance** we feel a sense of security, feeling abundant, secure, and grounded in the world. We feel safe, a feeling of being at home in our body and we have a strong connection with our Earth Mother that gives us a strong sense of belonging and connectedness. We feel balanced and rooted.

When **out of balance** we feel disconnected from our Mother Earth, feel ungrounded, exhibit feelings of insecurity both in terms of our physical safety and a lack of financial security and abundance. We may exhibit feelings of abandonment derived from childhood, which is very common. We can hold abuse trauma in this chakra as well as our Sacral Chakra that is also affected. Connecting with our great Mother Earth can help us let go of old insecurities and feel safe and grounded.

Sacred Trees

The sacred trees of Earth stand tall and proud. They are the Silent Ones offering us our essential oxygen and absorbing our carbon dioxide. Along with plants they are part of Earth's medicine, providing healing elixirs, wood, shelter, our fruit, and berry harvests. They hold much wisdom about life on Earth. They often live for hundreds of years, being witness to centuries of human evolution; they are often here before we are born and live long after we have left these earthly planes.

If you are like me and love trees, you'll find me on a slow walk through some woods, opening my heart to say hello and connect to the trees, hugging them, touching their bark, marvelling at their magnificence, wishing to know their inner secrets of longevity, strength, and endurance. They stand in all weathers, surrendering to what comes – if only we could let go so bravely and easily as they do!

In shamanic medicine, trees act as a portal for heaven and earth. I know when I lead shamanic journeys it is a sacred tree that sometimes comes forward to offer its wisdom and is a portal to the upper and lower worlds where much healing and wisdom reside.

I have worked closely with a few trees, and here are three I would love to share with you for Winter.

Sacred Oak

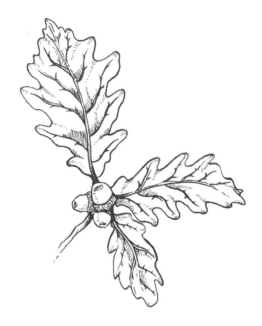

The magnificence of the Sacred Oak is a favourite for many people with its wide strong trunk with its deep roots in the history and myths of many cultures.

According to the Woodland Trust, Oaks may live for 1,000 years, although 600 may be more typical on many sites. All oak is classed as ancient from 400 years onwards, although many will have ancient characteristics from around 300 years. Typically, a veteran oak is 150-300 years of age.

The Oak is a sacred tree to the Druids and our Celtic ancestors, having performed many gatherings and rituals to celebrate and give thanks under the canopy of the tree's shelter. Many believed that King Arthur's round table was made of a single piece of Oak.

It was also a prominent tree growing in Roman sacred groves, seemingly having a link to Zeus the God of Sky, Thunder, and Lightning. It has a huge tap root like a spear or lightning rod that is rammed into the Earth. It is also known as a doorway between the worlds of spirit and matter.

The Sacred Oak is a symbol of longevity and strength, being home to many different species of insects and spiders. The Oak is believed to feed many species including pigs that are sacred to the Mother Goddess particularly Cerridwen, a Welsh Goddess of the Dark (we explore Cerridwen in *Chapter 12 Our Inner Cave and Sanctuary*).

The Oak's acorns carry the blueprint of the mother tree, where the saying 'mighty oaks from little acorns grow' comes from.

Sacred Oak Wisdom

Inner Strength – it pushes into existence with tremendous force
Strong Masculine energy
Endurance and Longevity
Courage
Provider

Bach Flower Remedy:

Oak is good for protection, grounding, and gives courage when going through change and transition.

Connecting with Oak

Walk up slowly to an Oak tree, with your heart open begin to feel the edges of its energy and life force and where it meets yours. Slow down your breathing to match the quietness of the Oak. Pause and receive the spirit of the Oak with gratitude. You may feel a natural merging of your energy fields if you are sensitive to feel this.

Sit or place a hand on its trunk and be with its magnificence. Allow it to speak to you through the heart, share any problem or question you need help with. As you sit for a while, you may notice you begin to absorb its mighty life force. You may receive ideas or inspiration. You may like to ask permission to enter through an invisible doorway and allow the Sacred Oak to take you on a healing journey. You can do this in person or remotely. Remember to always honour your connection by leaving a sacred offering.

Making a Wand

You might find a fallen piece of branch or twig with which to make a wand. Its strong life force can help you connect with your inner strength and power. You may like to plane your piece of wood with sandpaper (you can purchase varies depths of thickness depending on your desired effect you want to create). You can then decorate with feathers and stones with a hole in that can be tied to the stick, and beads of different colours.

Collect Acorns as a symbol of abundance and strength and lay them in your Winter Sacred Space as a representation of the promise to come.

My Communion with Oak

Today I stood with my spine supported by Sacred Oak.

I asked:

What wisdom do you wish to share with me today?

"When you flow with the rhythm of the Universe, all the answers you seek come to you easily.

Dear Child, let go.

All can be found within.

All that you seek is within your heart, for here resides the Universe.

What is your heart's deepest desire?"

(Pause)

"Receive yourself.

Be all that you are in this moment.

Accept.

All will unfold from here.

Be patient.

Just as I know Spring follows Winter, know your time will come in the promise of a new bud."

Such gentle strength flowed as I received these words. I gave my gratitude to the great Oak and felt his gentle strength in my heart flow with me the rest of the day.

Often, we seek answers and clarity outside of ourselves, thinking another knows better.

The Sacred Oak guides us back to the strength within, to discover our own answers.

Holly

We all know Holly with its bright red berries in autumn and winter. Evergreen Holly is another masculine tree with a potent life force. It thrives in woods and can be found amongst the shady canopy of Oak and other tall trees. It grows slowly demonstrating that it has patience and the wisdom to know where it is going thus it helps with life direction. You only have to look at the way its central branches grow up straight from the base of the ground, to see this in action. It is made from tough, hard wood and when sanded down it reveals a beautiful white wood.

According to *The Spirit of Trees* by Fred Hageneder, they can reach 250-300 years. They display small white flowers in May and June and bright red berries hang from their branches in autumn that remain throughout Winter as important food for birds. There are separate male and female trees that are often growing close together to aid pollination.

Holly Wisdom

Unconditional Love
Restores balance and life direction
Protection
Strength of heart
Unification of Heart and Mind.

Bach Flower Remedy:

Holly is a protective remedy against anything which is not unconditional love. It helps heal and open the heart helping to unify past hurts and trauma, bringing you into a place of forgiveness and balance in the present moment.

Connecting with Holly

Being a protective tree, it was considered unlucky to cut down. It might be possible to use any broken or fallen branches to make a wand. If you do feel called to take a branch do so only when given permission, approaching the tree with love and respect. Feel the answer with your heart and honor what you receive even if this means walking away and leaving it until another time. Always leave a sacred offering of thanks and gratitude such as flowers, herbs, crystal or stone or sacred spring water. This is a wonderful way to develop a strong bond between you.

I was fortunate to find a partly broken branch in the New Forest, Hampshire, whilst walking in the woods one winter. I had decided I wanted to make a wand and this piece of Holly reached out to me.

Setting up my sacred space at home, with intention, I enjoyed some hours sanding the wood down until it was smooth and had begun to reveal the beautiful white wood. It is a lovely way to learn the power of unconditional love. As I spent time with the Holly energy, I received lots of downloads of heat and warmth down through my crown to my heart. It stayed in my Healing Room for a few years before I felt called to decorate it with brightly coloured ribbons reflecting the five sacred elements and a little bell to bring in the gentle power of Sound. I am sure this is something I will add to as the years pass, weaving in the magic of life's wonder.

I also made a Talking Stick out of Holly. Again, as I ceremonially sanded it down, I received lots of energy and heat that began to inform the shape and form of what I was creating in my hands.

As I stood back, I could see the end of the piece of wood took the shape of a certain animal. First, I thought it was a Dragon and then it shapeshifted to become the head of a magical Seahorse with a Dolphin fin riding just behind. I adorned it with seagull feathers – bringing in their high-pitched cries and their ability to soar high and be very vocal. I also looped some colourful turquoise beads reminiscent of the ocean.

I then dedicated the Talking Stick with a Sacred Prayer of Intent. I called on the five elements of Earth, Air, Fire, Water and Great Spirit to ask for their blessings, especially the element of Air to assist us with speaking our authentic truth. I also asked the Holly to share its wisdom and strength.

What is so magical about this is I did not plan how I wanted it to look, it materialised through my open heart and whilst co-creating with Holly.

Consider what you would like to create in Winter. Is there a tree that calls you? I invite you on one of your Winter walks to see what tree and pieces of wood you find. Hold the intention of wanting to get to know the gifts of a particular tree or that you want to find a piece of wood good for making a Wand, a talisman or to become a Feather Wand.

Elder

Elder is a tree of regeneration and healing. Its wood contains a soft white pitch. It has creamy white flowers in June and early autumn she shares black juicy berries long known for its healing medicine rich in Vitamin C. Elderberry syrup made from the berries strengthens the immune system and making preserves of juice and elderberry jam is a fun way to connect with her deep medicine.

Elder is a protective benevolent tree and is associated with the Elder Woman and Goddess associated with death and rebirth. She is considered to hold the energy of a wise old woman and the Crone, guardian of the crossing of thresholds to the underworld, death, and the dark inner mysteries. With her medicine, she sooths fears and brings us gently through the dark tunnel to the Light, helping us to see the beginning in every ending.

Elder Wisdom

Death and Rebirth
Regeneration
Magic of Renewal
Elder/Crone Wisdom

Connecting with Elder

If you have an Elder tree near you, you might like to gather some of the berries to make Elderberry syrup or some jam. Alternatively, a piece of her wood that you can place in your Sacred Space is a reminder of the wisdom and magic of the never ending cycle of death and rebirth.

Call on the spirit of Elder to support you in letting go, helping you to see the wisdom of the dark phase and that renewal comes from every ending, providing something more beneficial and purposeful.

You can find out more about setting up your sacred space in *Chapter 9: Creating Sacred Space*.

Sacred Offerings

When we connect with trees or plants or sacred sites, it is important to honour their wisdom and show our appreciation by leaving an offering of love and gratitude. If you know you are going to a sacred site or on a mindfulness walk, go prepared. Collect some flowers or dried lavender, perhaps carry a small bottle of blessed spring water. You can also leave a crystal or stone as an offering. Hold them in your hand and say out loud, or if you prefer quietly to yourself, a prayer of love and thanks before leaving it at the base of the tree or a little nook or hollow where the fairies reside. Be open to the sensation of the wind and the rustle of leaves, as often trees will respond with a gentle breeze or rush of wind. Sometimes a bird will call at significant points. Listen with an open heart and feel the magic of Nature all around you.

Sacred Earth Exercises

Clear Your Energy

Use some of the techniques suggested in *chapter 8: Feminine Self-Nourishment Practices*, including smudging using sacred herbs, visualising white light to cleanse and replenish.

Use the **Grounding Meditation** below to anchor your roots into the Earth.

Grounding Meditation

Focusing your breath into your womb and belly. Then take your breath down your legs into your feet and toes.

Plant your feet firmly on the ground. Breathe out into the ground beneath you.

Imagine you have strong roots growing out from your hips and the souls of your feet (imagine a strong Oak or Beech tree) that go deep into the Earth beneath you.

Feel and visualise your roots following the roots of the tree, moving deeper and deeper through the structures of the inner Earth, following the flows of the underground rivers and streams.

Intend that your roots go deep into the Heart of Mother Earth, Gaia and her diamond light centre and emerald, green heart. Anchor your roots here and allow Mother Earth to hold and love you. Rest here a few minutes in her peaceful heart.

When you are ready, breathe her life force up your roots, as if you are drinking her sap to replenish your body. Feel her move through your veins, blood, and bones, strengthening them, breathing her deep into your womb and belly to energise and replenish. And then up into your heart. Feel her love.

Allow your heart to open and soften, expanding your capacity to receive as well as give. As your heart expands, your crown at the top of your head begins to gradually open to reveal a beautiful Lotus flower.

Feel your connection with the Moon, the Sun, and the Stars in the Cosmos.

Breathe in the starlight and let it fall into your heart.

Breathe, relax, and let go.

Sit and bathe in these energies until you feel balanced and replenished.

You may wish to listen to my Guided Meditation 'Connect and Ground:'

Mindful Nature Walk

Connect with Earth's Winter cloak – discover the beauty of her nakedness, what is decaying and composting down. Notice how she mirrors certain aspects in your own life. Learn to love this natural part of the cycle. Feel her raw primal power in the wind that blows, in the rain that falls, in the wild oceans that crash on the shore. Enjoy the peace and stillness of snow-covered hills and mountains, and the strength of the bare trees that endure all weathers, and the dazzling crisp of frosty mornings that create sculptures of art and beauty. Watch how the animals and birds forage in the winter. What can you learn from them?

Connect with a favourite tree or a tree that calls you. Stand with your spine against its trunk and feel is strength run down your spine. Feel your feet planted deeply, feeling your roots journey with the roots of the tree.

Collect material, or wood that represents something that is dying or falling away in your life. Use to either burn ceremonially or to contemplate and work with over the winter months before burying it with prayer and thanks for the healing and wisdom the tree has given you.

Create Your Own Medicine Wheel with Stones

Work with stone, creating a medicine wheel inside your home or outside. Collect five stones – these can be relatively small. Place them in a circle working with the sacred elements of Earth, Air, Fire Water and Great Spirit in the centre. If you are able to use the compass, mark these according to their direction (Earth/North, Air/East, Fire/South and Water/West and Great Spirit in the centre of your circle). Discover more in *Chapter 9: Creating Sacred Space* at the end of Part One.

Work with **ceremonial bones**. If you have found any small bones left by dead animals or feathers dropped on your path, take these to your sacred space to work with over Winter. Give thanks to the spirit of the animal or bird.

What message do they bring you?

What do they symbolise in your life?

Tune in during meditation and while sitting within your Medicine Wheel to discover the wisdom of what you have found and how it may support you through Winter.

Earth's Sacred Medicine – Cacao

Since ancient times Cacao has been used as a medicine to heal physical, mental, and spiritual illnesses. Made from raw Cacao beans she is used to make a medicine healing drink that has a slight bitter taste. It is deeply healing and heart opening. The Spirit of Mamma Cacao has been shown to boost the immune system and lower cholesterol and blood pressure as well as leading to euphoria and deeper spiritual connection. Cacao is a beautiful healing plant medicine, helping us to open our hearts to receive a deeper connection with Mother Earth and Great Spirit.

Some of Cacao's amazing benefits include:

- Theobromine stimulates the cardiovascular system helping us to feel calm and clear.
- Contains tryptophan, a natural precursor to the neurotransmitter serotonin which lifts mood.
- Contains dopamine, 'the pleasure neurotransmitter,' that increases concentration, focus and mental clarity.
- One of the richest sources of antioxidants that reduces free radicals.
- Contains high levels of magnesium, copper, zinc, iron, calcium, manganese, sulphur and phosphorous, to balance our emotional and physical wellbeing.
- Regulates blood pressure and blood sugar.
- Enhances meditative states.
- Opens our heart, helping us to express and receive love more easily.
- Induces a feeling of peace and 'all is well.' Some people feel Cacao induces a state of bliss.

It can be used to drink during the day but is best used ceremonially to get the best out of the experience. In *Chapter 9: Creating Sacred Space* I share more of how you can create a beautiful healing experience with Mamma Cacao.

Journal Prompts

Where are you rooted in the past? What dead roots are ready to be dug up or pruned?

What do you feel and know deep in your bones?

What feelings does Winter evoke for you?

How does Mother Earth in her Winter cloak reflect what is going on in your life?

What elements of your life are ready to die and fall away?

How can you connect more deeply with Mother Earth during Winter?

CHAPTER 6

Feminine Inner Seasons

Women's Inner Seasons and Cycles

In the previous chapters, we discussed the Spiral of Life and the Wheel of the Year and how we exist as part of the continual cycle of life.

We now spiral inwards to discover our own unique seasons and cyclical nature, a pathway that will lead us back to our source of feminine power and inner wisdom.

Within our own menstrual cycle, we experience the same fluid movement that makes up the inner seasons of Winter, Spring, Summer, and Autumn. These are our expressions of the continual cycle of death and rebirth. Women's unique design means we are best placed to understand and embody the true nature and power of our Mother Creator.

It is useful to know that we experience these cycles within the context of our whole life's journey, known as Life Phases or transitions, that offer an opportunity for initiation and powerful rites of passage, as we move from one stage and phase of our life to the next. We may recognise these phases as:

- Birth (when we incarnate into this Earthly life),
- Childhood
- Puberty
- Motherhood
- Wild Woman/Enchantress
- Wise Crone/Elder; this last phase being the culmination of our life's wisdom.

As we live in flow with the rhythms of the Earth, we discover our own way to honour and trust our inner cycles. These inner cycles become the voice of our intuitive knowing and inner wise counsel. With practice, we learn to understand our own body's unique sensations and feelings and what they mean to each of us, guiding us to live in harmony with the ebb and flow of the Universe.

Our Menstrual Cycle

"Women are the archetypal anchors for the power of the Feminine, and when we reclaim our feminine power – by restoring our ways and practices – we integrate the power of the Feminine into our lives and back on to the planet. Our ways as women are the embodied practice of the menstrual cycle awareness. As each woman works with and trusts in its process and power, she develops an initiation of the Sacred Feminine."

'Wild Power' by Alexandrea Pope and Sjanie Hugo Wurlitzer*

Wild Power written by Alexandra Pope and Sjanie Hugo Wurlitzer, Founders of Red School, has been a source of great wisdom and inspiration for me on my journey.

From the centre of our own being, our womb space, we have the power to sow the seeds of our dreams to co-create with the power of the Universe.

Our womb's menstrual cycle is our inner guide and map for reconnecting with our inherent and potent creative power. It is a woman's greatest gift, as when we deepen in and trust our inner cycle and flow with it, it offers us great power and choice. It allows us to flow with what is and accept when to rest and incubate our ideas, and when is the perfect time to create and move forwards.

Our cycle is a perfect reflection of how we experience seasons within the natural world, becoming part of our inner journey. When we are in tune with Nature's rhythms, we see ourselves in Nature's reflection, naturally deepening into the source of our own being that sustains our vitality.

Whether we still experience a bleed, have a physical womb or not, we still connect with the powerful energy of our etheric womb space. Some women report still experiencing bodily sensations and symptoms as if they were having an actual bleed and this has certainly been my experience going through the perimenopause and menopause phase of my life. We have the capacity to tune into the wisdom of our womb cycle through deep listening and trust in our body consciousness that allows us to make positive choices that are aligned with our highest good.

Womb Map and Your Inner Seasons

In the Womb Map, we can see how the inner seasons of our menstrual cycle are mirrored by Nature's seasons.

The Map of the Inner Seasons of the menstrual cycle was originally developed by Alexandra Pope and Sjanie Hugo Wurlitzer of Red School but has been adapted for the purposes of this book.

The **Womb Map** shows the seasons of our inner Winter, Spring, Summer, and Autumn. We know we are greatly influenced by the magnetic power and gravitational pull of the Moon, and I have therefore included the Full and New Moon phases within the Womb Map.

I have included the Moon cycle of the New/Dark Moon and Full Moon as an expression of the Winter and Summer phases respectively, but this does not mean your menstrual cycle has to fit within that.

I have noticed over the years how my bleed would for many years be around the Full Moon and then it gradually shifted to the New Moon during my perimenopause phase of life. Each woman's cycle is unique to her. There is no right or wrong way to be. Honour her flow.

There are many things that influence our menstrual cycle, along with the Moon cycles and so we need to be mindful of taking a holistic approach that makes up who we are. We are dynamic beings and at the centre of our true Feminine Nature, we are chaotic, changeable, and wild.

Some of the factors that may influence our menstrual cycle include:

- Our hormonal balance
- Our relationship with our body
- What we inherit from our parents through our DNA
- Our lifestyle and levels of stress
- What age and stage we are in our life ie, motherhood, pregnancy, irregular periods, child loss, perimenopause and menopause.

We are guided to tune in and listen. There is no right or wrong way to experience our cycle. What is important is to live in harmony and acceptance of oneself.

If we have irregular periods or uncomfortable or painful periods, or have physical symptoms such as fibroids, ovarian cysts and the painful condition of endometriosis, then this Menstrual Map is one way we can begin to tune in and listen to what our body may be telling us and what changes we may need to make to our lifestyle that can help heal, including:

- How we deal with and manage stress,
- Our diet,
- The quality of our relationship with ourself and others (past relationships or situations that we are energetically still attached to),
- Our emotional, mental, and physical health and wellbeing.

This guidance should not replace the seeking of professional help and treatment from your doctor or GP but should be considered alongside it so that you can become more informed.

Our menstrual cycle is our barometer and inner guidance to our overall state of health. Understanding and knowing our true nature by following our inner cycles creates harmony, balance, and vitality in our lives.

We journey through a typical monthly cycle of between 21-28 days and we experience our inner seasons just as Mother Nature intended.

Inner Winter (Yin) – Our Wise Woman/Crone Archetype

"When I bleed, I am in full flow with my Feminine Power and my connection to the wisdom of the Earth brings me home to Self."

We begin the Wheel of the Year with the season of Winter, as a reflection of the void in which we find ourselves – the powerful cauldron of transformation, for death and renewal and the birthing of the new.

Our Inner Winter is also our time of bleed and is a potent time for us to tune in, let go of old patterns, emotions, and heaviness we have accumulated during the previous cycle.

Just like in the Earthly season of Winter when we want to hibernate, many of us want to close the door on the external world so that we may listen and nurture our inner world. In Inner Winter we are encouraged to slow down, rest and reorganise our schedule so that we can go about our day slowly and gently. We feel more sensitive and vulnerable to external influence, so it is natural for us to seek inner refuge away from the noise of the external world. It is important to create space to rest, heal and nourish oneself rather than to push through to avoid letting other people down. Otherwise, we end up letting ourselves down. We deserve better.

Once you become aware of your Cycle you can begin to reorganise your diary to create more space and time for yourself during this phase.

This is a good time to get a diary specifically for mapping out your menstrual flow.

Inner Spring - Maiden

'Just like a seed that needs to have the right conditions of soil, rain and sunshine to flower and flourish, I need the right conditions within to fully blossom.'

Towards the end of our bleed, we may feel the tentative signs of wanting to venture out into the world again. Our focus gently shifts externally, bringing with it a freshness of spirit and a feeling of new adventure. Just like the young Maiden as she ventures out with playful curiosity and wonder, we may feel the spirit of our inner child and young teenager emerging. We see through eyes of wonder and imagination, wanting to try out and play with new ideas that have been surfacing during the winter period of introspection. There is a sense of rejuvenation, just like we feel when we emerge from Earth's Winter into the energy of Spring with its new growth.

This is a gradual process and the more we have been able to slow down and surrender to our Inner Winter to feel held and nourished, the more likely we are ready to move on and embrace life again in Spring.

To avoid an overwhelm of ideas, it is important to pace ourselves and not to think we need to implement every creative idea that we have received. Our Inner Spring is a time to explore and play with ideas and then to prioritise what is important for us to focus on.

Some ideas we receive are inspiration for what is to come, which may be months or even years before they land and manifest fully.

Inner Summer (Yang) - Motherhood

'Summer is where I feel I am at one with Nature's bounty. I am in full flow expressing my essence and fragrance for all to enjoy.'

When experiencing our Inner Summer, we tend to feel in a state of expansion, our self and our projects are blossoming. It is the time of ovulation, the ripening of growth. Just like Nature's Summer, during this phase we are likely to be in full flow with life and feel expansive. We may feel this is a time of celebration as we successfully express ourself out in the world, dancing with the rhythm of life herself.

Summer is the active 'doing' Yang phase and so we generally want to be out having fun, feeling connected to friends, family, and life's abundance.

Some women at ovulation feel physically tender and sensitive, we are each unique. Keep listening to your body's needs and if this occurs make sure you are eating the right foods for you, such as plenty of fruit and vegetables to help clear the system of water retention and slowing down and paying attention to what your body needs is helpful.

Inner Autumn – Enchantress, Wild Woman

'Wild and free, I am like the wind and sea, one day calm, another day wild and powerful, yet I am rooted in my knowing.'

Autumn is a time to review and reflect on the cycle that has just been. What has worked well, spending time reflecting on our achievements, embracing our inner harvest and celebrating them.

As part of this period of reflection, this phase offers space for the wild 'inner critic' to surface. This can have a mixed energy if our inner critic is too harsh, and we can create our own undermining energy that affects our self-esteem. Her intention as the wise inner critic is, in fact, to begin to identify what needs to be pruned back, as she prepares for us to let go in the Winter phase once again. You may find that you do become more vocal as your inner truth surfaces. Your Wild Woman/ Enchantress phase may give you the energy and empowerment you need to speak those words and truth that has been previously bottled up.

We may also begin to display feelings of irritability with other people and have feelings of frustrations as our raw nature can be wild and chaotic at this time. If so, it is time to heed the call to go within to discover what needs and support She requires, so that her frustrations don't spill out or project on to those close around you.

Self-nourishment is a quality many women do not feel comfortable with and yet is essential to navigate this phase. We need a balance of giving and receiving as too often, we may tend to over deliver and put others needs before our own. Replenishing ourselves and having clear boundaries around our own physical and energetic space is important.

Self-nourishment practices are given at the end of Part One. Developing a daily nourishment practice can offer a solid foundation which can support us especially when life gets challenging. We have something to fall back on; just like a tank of petrol, those inner reserves of energy that give you hope and inner resilience to get through life's struggles.

The Menopause Phase

At the end of our fertile years, at the time of menopause, we can experience this Autumn phase. During Autumn we naturally reflect on the past year and at this stage in our life of perimenopause, we are likely to revisit our early teenage years, our inner Maiden, the time of our first bleed as our bodies begin to come full circle. There are likely to be matters that come to our attention for healing and resolution especially around our sexuality and identity as a young woman.

This is the phase I have been in for the few years of writing this book which has proven to be a powerful rite of passage for me. Moving beyond the roles that I have performed as mother, daughter, sister, wife, to becoming the real me, independent, expressing my wild sensual nature has been a delicious outcome of moving through this phase. And I am still learning and evolving as I dive deeper into the wildness of who I am.

It has not been without its challenges. Physically, I experienced a lot of night sweats, hot flushes – this is our power rising so welcome her – burning off the old conditioning – with migraines and purging at times. So not the most comfortable of experiences but I stuck with it, with her, as I knew the real me was emerging through this. For physical symptoms homeopathy and acupuncture really helped me through this transition.

Emotionally and spiritually seeking support from my healing therapist was important, and going slowly was a must. Old sexual inhibitions and insecurities surfaced for healing. As a teenager I didn't feel confident to express my sexuality for fear of being out of control, for fear of judgement – a common issue amongst women. In our teens we are most sensitive as we transition to being a young woman. I wished I had the hand-holding during this vital phase to honour the powerful wisdom of my menstrual cycle and my feminine sexuality. If you have young daughters moving through their teenage years to young womanhood, I hope this information will help them to become more aware of their own power as Woman. I am excited to share more of my sexual journey with you in my Summer Spiral book.

* * *

It is fascinating that we have such a powerful source of inner wisdom and guidance to draw upon. Many of us have been brought up to ignore, deny or see the menstrual cycle as an inconvenience or a curse. We have lost the sacred meaning and power of our cycle that is intrinsically linked to our creative power to manifest a joyful and authentic life. We have become too focussed on the external world for validation and power that we have neglected our own powerful resource within us.

Even though I no longer have a monthly bleed, I still feel the gentle swelling of my belly when I move into my inner autumn/winter phase and then a release. I still use this time for inner counsel, to realign with what is true and important to me. Personally, I align with the Dark of the New Moon, my Inner Winter and Crone energy, to go within, rest and replenish.

Understanding the wisdom of your own cycle and needs during these times is invaluable in creating more flow, vitality and joy in your life. One the next page are some journal questions to support your reflection and the changes you may like to make.

Journal Prompts

Tuning into Your Menstrual Cycle

- Make a Moon and menstrual diary and note down your menstrual cycle and where it falls in relation to the Moon cycle. There are many Apps you can find online and for your phone that you can use to identify the patterns so that you can begin to make better choices about how you live your life.
- Notice when your bleed normally happens – does it fall on or near the New or Full Moon?
- How do you feel at these points in your cycle?
- Can you allow yourself more space in your daily schedule for the days when you bleed when you may need to rest and slow down? Remember we can feel very tired during this time, and it is better to surrender than push through, as there are consequences to our choices that impact the rest of our cycle.
- Notice in which parts of your cycle do you feel most energised and when you feel most tired?
- Plan your creative phase around the times you feel most energised and reorganise deadlines and fitness regimes to fit more comfortably around your inner cycle.
- If your periods are irregular, note down when they do occur and what your activity/rest levels are like during the periods in between.
- What correlations are there between your lifestyle and when you bleed? Was there a time when they were regular and what happened when they became irregular?
- For those going through the perimenopause and menopause, note down your bleed and Inner Winter phase points in your diary. What do you notice in relation to the Moon cycles? In my experience, I became more sensitive to foods, to the environment and people. What extra support can you give yourself? How can you honour this important phase in your life and slow down to allow your body to adjust?

Journal Prompts – Life Phases

We have explored our Inner Seasons earlier in this chapter. We can experience these seasons as stages that occur through our whole life.

For me, whilst finishing this book, I have been in the Autumn and Winter season of my life during my menopause, as I gradually surrendered to the wild woman and wise elder of the community.

This rite of passage is something all women naturally go through and needs time, acknowledgement, and celebration to fully value the importance of these endings and new beginnings. This is an exciting time when we get to embrace the radiance of our authentic, wild, free She Power and Womanhood. Let's celebrate this phase rather than see ourselves as coming to the end of our time. We are coming into our prime.

Take a moment to reflect on your life and what phase of life you feel you are at.

Perhaps you are in transition or crossover between life phases. Use these journal prompts to aid your reflection. Alternatively, you may feel inclined to express yourself through drawing or painting, using colour, form and shape to express your inner most feelings.

I find sketching is one of my favourite ways to quickly capture my feelings and visions. Sometimes, I find these speak louder than words. I allow my heart to guide the pencil and create different shapes and forms. It is not about being an artist, this is about allowing your soul and heart to express through you. Enjoy.

1. What are the key dominant feelings you are experiencing at this stage in your life?
2. What are your thoughts and feelings that you experience?
3. If you are at a crossroads or in transition, ask yourself –
    How do you feel about the phase you are leaving?
    How do you feel about the new phase you are moving into?
4. What would make your life easier?
5. What support do you have around you to help you through your transition?
6. What additional support would you like?
7. What steps can you take to reach out for more support?
8. Beyond the roles of mother, daughter, sister, wife, carer, ask yourself:
    Who am I and Who am I becoming?

Learn to nourish and support yourself and deepen your connection with Mother Earth so you feel more deeply held and supported through change.

Use the information in the *Creating Sacred Space* chapter 9 to help you acknowledge and celebrate the ending and new beginnings of life and to help you transition with ease and grace.

CHAPTER 7:
Womb Wisdom

Why is the Womb so Important in Reclaiming Our Feminine Power?

The womb is the powerhouse of our creative energy. She is the container for our primal life force and in Chinese Medicine the womb (or hara in men) is considered our second power centre and brain.

She is the Keeper of all life, the Cauldron of death and rebirth, she is the source of our full feminine expression. Whether this is giving birth to physical children or what is often called 'children projects,' all seeds are sown within the fertile energy of the womb. It is through her that we connect with the Womb of the Earth and the Cosmic Womb, with its infinite pool of potentiality.

A woman's centre doesn't exist within the mind but within her navel and womb. We know that when we live in the head, the mind takes over with spiralling thoughts that take us away from our inner wisdom.We become top heavy, driven by logical thinking, competing with others for success and attention. In doing so, we lose touch with our deepest feminine knowing and intuition that is a felt experience within the body, specifically the centre of our pelvic region, the womb herself.

Many women have adopted a more masculine approach that is driven from a need to achieve and progress up the career ladder, adapting themselves to fit in with a patriarchal egoic society, driven by the need for control, greed and power over others. There are many women who work and are successful in their career, but I wonder at what cost to their overall health and wellbeing? They may continue to strive, living off adrenaline, but on a deeper, perhaps unconscious level, there may be a niggle or restlessness as if something doesn't feel in balance. Their feminine needs and desires for flow, creativity, sensual expression and softness may be suppressed, creating long-term health issues, as they have lost the deeper connection with who they truly are as a woman. That soft compassionate, restful and often wild feminine is misunderstood and often left outside the boardroom for another time or ignored all together. But She is calling, She is rising. It is our time. There is another way to live a successful life that embraces both our authentic feminine and masculine needs.

As soon as our focus shifts to our womb, we become empowered, centred, and grounded in our power and in the knowledge of who we truly are. This connection provides a solid foundation for us to build a joyful, abundant, purposeful and vibrant life.

Women are the barometer for the state of our planet. Where society has placed more value on the 'old' masculine principle of 'doing' that controls the outcome focussed on achievement alone, we've ignored the importance of the 'being' phase, the way of the feminine and her flow, to create with ease. As more women awaken and move beyond what is considered culturally acceptable for them to be, there will be a shift in all men and women and our relationship with the Earth.

In the Yin and Yang symbol, we can see the need for light and dark; the light of the Yang (masculine) energy that impregnates the energy of the dark, Yin (feminine) energy. One cannot exist without the other.

All life will benefit when women begin to heal and remember to honour and trust their bodies as a sacred temple of power and truth.

Returning to Our Womb

Womb Breathing

Knowing all this, let us pause for a moment. Let me invite you to do some womb breathing with me. Just five minutes is all it takes to begin a new relationship with yourself.

Take a deep breath in and then a long exhalation and sigh out. Do this a few times to relax.

Let everything else go as you bring your full attention to yourself and the present moment.

Settle yourself down in to your chair planting your feet on the ground or floor.

Gently place your left hand on your belly and your right hand on your heart.

Feel your breath drop down into your belly. Take some gentle deep breaths here.

Continue to place your attention on your breath in your belly.

Breathe just under your hand as it lies on your belly. Feel your belly rise and fall with each breath.

Focus your breath inwards as if you are connecting with the womb space herself.

Focus on opening your heart to receive Her.

Feel what you feel, notice what you notice.

Warmth, coolness, sensations, energy moving.

Numbness, pain, sadness, fear, anger, joy, and pleasure

and nothing.

All is welcome, without judgement.

Honour what you feel with compassion and gratefulness.

Listen and allow and rest here a while.

When you are ready, take a couple of deep breaths.

Bring your awareness to the chair you are sitting on, and your feet planted on the ground.

Become aware of the room you are in.

Gently open your eyes and adjust to your surroundings.

It may feel unusual and slightly uncomfortable at first as you breathe into your belly, particularly if you normally breathe higher up in your chest.

You may like to note down any observations in your journal – note how you feel.

See if you can keep a gentle connection with your womb for the rest of the day.

You may like to draw upon the *Meditation* resources on my website, a link can be found under Resources at the back of the book.

When we start connecting with our womb, deep emotions can surface, connecting us to the neglect and judgement we have received over many years and lifetimes of suppression. Cleansing and healing the wounds of separation, the energy of hate, judgement and shame that has taken up root in our womb space, is a powerful reclamation of our rightful power. Through the love of our heart, we listen, forgive, and embrace all that we are and bring ourselves home. We return to the Mother of All.

Reconnecting with our womb space means we get to reclaim our She Power and wisdom and embody this place of womanhood, our source of joy. As we shift our attention to our womb, it allows the full expression of our feminine essence through the heart, allowing our heart to organically open and flower.

By doing so, we not only feel deeply nourished, but we bring balance and healing to all men, as it heals the many deep-seated wounds that are held in both the female and male consciousness. As women heal their mistrust of the 'wounded' masculine, our soft open heart can hold the masculine's place of vulnerability, with love and compassion. Men learn to reclaim their feminine essence and soften into their heart and so also come into balance.

This act of healing the male psyche requires a woman to be fully in her authentic power, to be able to receive her partner with an open and loving heart. If she still holds judgement, mistrust or fears the masculine, this will be consciously or unconsciously picked up by her partner, who then may feel unsafe to open his heart fully.

Often people assume that a soulmate relationship is all joy and happiness when in fact a true soulmate relationship offers the gift of deep transformation. Each partner acts as a mirror to our deeper patterns and behaviours, guiding us back to our sacred Soul. It requires authentic expression based on love and honesty, to be able to navigate the often, challenging path successfully. We are all on this journey, whether we consciously know it or not. It takes time and patience, compassion, and kindness. There is no-one fix for all problems. It is a journey along the various spirals of healing that come to us at the perfect time.

This has been my own experience with my husband, a journey of deep healing and relating. I notice as I personally make a big shift, further softening and opening my heart, I have noticed he responds differently, resulting in more harmony between us. With my wider family my healing journey has increasingly enabled me to rest in my core centre helping me to feel safe in my body to express my needs and desires and to honour my truth without feeling belittled like I may have done as a child. Sometimes it can trigger a challenging response in others, that requires me to stay in my centre, to honour my truth. It is always a learning experience and one that requires patience and compassion with self and each other.

What Does This Mean for Us Women?

It means releasing all the stored anger and judgement in relationship to the masculine so that we can receive our partner with love, trust, integrity without judgement, suspicion, or fear. It is the feminine fire of our heart/womb connection that holds the key for alchemy and transformation in all our heart-centred relationships and thus we heal the wounds that have been passed down from an unbalanced patriarchal society.

Having spent many years healing to embrace my sacred feminine and feeling very connected with her, I have been in recent years healing my 'wounded' masculine. It has been the power of my feminine heart to hold the grief of my masculine wounding, from past lives and that has come down our ancestral lineage, that has allowed beautiful alchemy to take place. I have experienced pain in the right side of my body and my right breast as I was healing, allowing the Divine Masculine and his authentic power to step in more fully.

As we ascend to higher levels of consciousness, our sacred feminine needs our sacred masculine to step up and be the protector and leader he is destined to be so that she can share her gifts and presence more confidently in the world. We bring balance and harmony in the world through healing and coming into harmony and union with our sacred feminine and sacred masculine.

Our womb is the foundation for honouring all life, hence the interconnection with the Cosmic Womb. When each one of us reclaims our authentic power, we come into a balanced and harmonious relationship with all Life.

Symptoms of Disconnection

As we now know, the womb stores the energetic imprint of every intimate encounter we have ever experienced and because of this the true power and voice of our womb is often distant or muffled. This affects the quality of our health, wellbeing and self-esteem as it becomes difficult to feel and see with clarity where our own energy begins, and another person's energy finishes. Wobbly boundaries are often a sign that the energy of our womb needs clearing and healing.

Healing Our Disconnection

What symptoms do you experience that may show a disconnection with your womb?

- Do you have painful, heavy, or irregular or no periods?
- Do you experience pain and discomfort in your hips and/or lower back?
- Have you ever had any disease or physical imbalance in your pelvic area, your belly, womb and sexual organs?
- Have you had any of the following? – Fibroids, ovarian cyst, cervical cancer, endometriosis, fertility problems or irregularities with your menstrual cycle?
- How aware and connected are you to your belly, womb, and sexual organs?
- Do you have low libido or sexual drive and passion?
- Do you suffer from PMS and hormonal imbalances?
- Do you tend to hide this part of your body feeling self-conscious or are you happy to flaunt your belly, hips, and breasts?
- What was your birth story? How do you feel about your birth?
- What is your mother's story about her body and sexuality?
- Have you suffered sexual, emotional or physical abuse in your life?
- How easy or difficult do you find it is for you to express yourself and stand up for your views and opinions with confidence?
- Do you tend to say yes when you really want to say no?
- Do you find you have wobbly boundaries, choosing to waver depending on the person or influence of another? Such as, allowing another person's energy to infiltrate your own so that you are less able to hear your own inner voice with clarity.

Clearing the Way to Hear Our Inner Voice

Often the first step on our spiritual path is to open our hearts and higher chakras through a process of engaging in meditation and mindfulness. However, without a strong foundation, the heart does not feel safe to fully open and flower. We become out of balance.

The journey now is for us to go deeper into the true self, to ground and embody our path with the Earth so we can rise with our power fully activated and connected both above and below.

We need to unlearn and unravel all the programming and conditioning, and listen to the voice of our inner world; clear away the external noise to create greater depths of knowing, intuition, self-love and acceptance. This naturally allows the energy of our womb to flow, giving birth to creative projects, vibrant health, partnerships, and abundance in all areas of our life.

Our womb's voice is ancient, wise and powerful and she may challenge us to choose different pathways than the mind would choose. However, when we fully learn to trust again in our inner knowing we know this is the right call.

Through my own experience, I have found the womb has her own unique and sweet voice that is encouraging, empowering, and affirming. When I really listen to her, she speaks to me in a language of sensations, a knowing sense, like a feeling of confirmation, strength, and power. Sometimes I hear her words, softly spoken, rise within me to my heart. Other times she wishes to express her emotions of sadness and hurt coming deep from within and released through tears or sobs. She may want to make sounds, soft whimpering sounds and other times loud ROARS (the throat is the higher expression of the womb and sacral chakra). There are times she wants to be quiet and still, and other times she wants to move and express herself through dance, opening the hips and shaking off any excess charge or tension she has absorbed through the day just like a wild animal.

What is most important is to allow her to be as She is, without control or judgement. We welcome everything that she brings. Gone are the times when she was controlled and ridiculed. NOW is the time to listen and allow her to express herself through the heart and allow her voice to be heard on the wind.

Interestingly, her voice is different to what I call my higher self's voice, as she has a different tone. My higher self comes through as inspiration that drops into my heart and mind from above. Whilst when my womb speaks, I often feel her voice rise from within me. Sometimes she speaks softly; other times she is demanding and bold. There is a subtle difference, something we each need to discover for ourselves.

When I have truly listened and trusted the knowing of my womb, I have allowed her to guide me in my choices and actions. Sometimes it requires patience, sitting in stillness until a clear answer comes. There are times in our lives that we experience what feels like periods of dormancy when we are not creating. Just like a field lies fallow for a year or so, the same can apply to us.

It is through my womb wisdom that I have been able to trust the creative process of life, knowing when to be patient and receptive and when to allow my masculine to move forwards into action, creating a beautiful dance between the feminine and masculine. This is when we know we are in our flow.

I know when I do not take the time to fully listen and allow my ego to take charge, it becomes a struggle and I feel stuck. Sometimes I have ended up pushing myself forwards when the time is not really in alignment with my best interests and the bigger plan.

For example, in birthing this book, She has had an energy and life force of her own. I have flowed with my own rhythm and the rhythmic pulse of the Earth. I have learnt to no longer push against my desire to have a particular result but to relax into the flow of what wants to be created in the moment. My womb knows her timing and what is perfect to birth this book. I have had to learn to tune in and align every day with my source of power and soul rather than listening to the critical egoic urges that pull me off track, distracting me from my true purpose.

The feminine is cyclical whilst the masculine is focussed and linear. In the example of my book, it is the masculine that gives structure and form, a safe container in which my feminine creativity can create and flow. Interestingly, I started with my writing rather than the structure. The structure came later but has changed several times to accommodate the flow of what wanted to be created. An example of how the balancing of the feminine and masculine energies can work together.

As we begin to clear our womb of all the noise of the external world our inner guidance becomes clear and precise. It is of course an organic process that takes time and lots of patience. Gradually with dedicated practice, our intuition becomes sharper, and we experience less hesitation in following our inner guidance.

Healing Our Womb

For many women and men, the pelvic area and hips carry a huge amount of unresolved emotions and trauma creating discomfort, tension, pain and numbness too, where we have buried our emotions and shut ourselves off from our sexual and primal life force.

The inner wisdom of the womb will never lie to us. She holds the energetic imprint of all our connections and relationships, sexual and otherwise and so everything felt and experienced is held at a cellular level.

Clearing the womb is the first step to reclaiming our authentic truth, power, and life's joyful expression.

As we journey deeper with the Earth cycles, you will be guided to a deeper level of awareness and understanding about your own womb.

Great Mother, Pachamama, has been my rock and foundation and my 'go to' place for comfort, love, and connection with myself. It is through a deepening into myself, in connection with Mother Earth, Gaia, that I welcome myself home in wholeness.

Sacred Commitment – Activating the Power of Our Womb

To heal and reactivate the power of our womb we must be dedicated to the journey of wanting to live a life of authenticity, of genuine feminine expression and be willing to embrace our shadow as well as our light. For when we claim our shadow, all the 'stuff' we have buried, we heal and transform and let go and embrace the lessons and teachings that become our greatest gifts and treasures. The shadow and light are who we are. In the darkness light is born.

'In the darkness light is born.'

Daily Commitment and Self-Awareness

A daily practice is one of the most powerful ways to awaken the womb and reclaim her wisdom. When we shift our attention to her with love and gratitude, we become anchored, more embodied, able to listen and hear our inner guidance and intuition clearly.

Are you ready to awaken your full feminine expression?

Are you ready to put yourself first and commit to a better life, healthier, more joyful, abundant and life full of vitality?

I hope now you feel enthusiastic and hopeful. Here is my experience of connecting with my womb I wish to share with you, followed by some Journal Prompts to explore your relationship with your womb.

Journal Entry - The Voice of My Womb

What does my womb want to say?

As part of my morning meditation, I got comfortable to sit quietly and connected deeply with my womb. I found this was a good practice to spend some time in meditation breathing with my womb to energise and connect with her power and wisdom. One day I decided to ask her what she wanted to share and this is what she said.

"Joy is my deep pleasure, my birthright, my gateway to bliss. Here is where I dwell in power, centred, home, a place of comfort and safety. It is for us (you and I) to choose who enters my space because I am the sacred container from which all life is born. It is from whence we came and to the belly of the Earth we will return.

Within the dark container of my chalice there is a gold waiting to birth, a gold of great richness you are yet to comprehend.

I am joy, I am the gift of life itself.

I journey with the laws of Nature not the laws of man.

I take the time and space I need to keep safe the seeds that we've sown, to nurture them, so they can gestate and give birth at the perfect time for all. Like a flower, I am unique and I have a unique time to reveal my creations for all to enjoy.

And this gold deep within me will rise to shine and sparkle like a prized jewel, for like a diamond I've been preparing this for many years and lifetimes.

I am your safe container.

When we deeply connect together in this way, heart to womb, I rise powerful ready to flower.

I am the fountain of your pleasure.

I am the passion that moves you.

I am joy in motion and in stillness.

I am the peace you seek in the well of forgiveness."

Journal Entry SSG 18/4/19

My womb is a sacred container
for JOY,
LOVE
and ABUNDANCE
to flourish.

Journal Prompts

1. How does it feel to begin connecting with your womb?

2. What rises up for you that needs honouring?

3. What physical sensations do you feel when you connect with your womb and pelvic region?

4. How can you begin to pay more attention to your body and her needs?

5. What does she want from you?

6. What does she wish to share with you?

7. How do these new realisations begin to affect the choices you make around your self-care?

Discover Guided Meditations for Womb Breathing and Healing on my website. Link at the back of the book under Resources and About the Author.

CHAPTER 8:
Feminine Self-Nourishment Practices

What it Means to Self-nourish

Creating space in our day and week for our self-care is so important for our general health and wellbeing. Imagine feeling nourished, relaxed, and calm.

What difference would that quality of feeling have on your levels of energy, your mood and therefore your relationships and your day?

Without continually replenishing our cup, we can become depleted physically and emotionally that can lead to disease and imbalance and health issues. When we are running on empty or half-full, we make poor choices, become irritable and tense and miss the magical synchronicity of life because we are out of alignment and not in our flow. People pick up on our energy and we may attract more arguments, stress, and tension in the long run.

The more you give time and space for your needs, to feel grounded and balanced, the more aligned your choices and actions are from your heart and soul. This calms the mind, helping incessant chatter to quieten, helping you make wiser choices that are aligned for your highest good.

Start to become aware of when your body is calling attention for some self-nourishment.

Is it a sensation you feel in your gut?

Do you feel a pain in your pelvic area?

Do you feel off balance and ungrounded?

Do you feel your energy fading?

Is there a niggle inside or do you sense the quiet, soft whispers of your heart?

Pausing in your day to connect inwards, to check in, to see what you need, is so important to how the rest of the day unfolds. Perhaps taking that break away from your laptop or taking that walk, is just what you need to clear your mind and refresh. Instead of pushing onwards with tasks, you may find that the walk gives you fresh inspiration or that you bump into someone you've not met for a long time that lifts your mood. Perhaps you are someone who likes to exercise, to take power walks, or go running, swim or go to the gym. Listen to what your body wants, not what you feel you should do.

Incorporate short breaks in your day, to refresh your energy levels and return with a new perspective ready to begin again, creating more ease and flow, and productivity in your day.

What does self-care and self-nourishment mean to you?

Connecting with Mother Nature

I love walking along by the shoreline where we live. Feeling the waves ebb and flow helps wash away the mental stresses and clears my mind. Sometimes I will paddle in the cool waters and ask Mother Sea to cleanse me and the winds to blow away the cobwebs. We can call on the elements of Nature to support our awakening and healing process. I also find water inspiring – it is where I get my biggest realisations and creative ideas. If you are not near the sea, can you get to a flowing stream or river or do the still waters of the lake call you?

We also need to remember we don't have to be on automatic pilot. We can gift ourselves days out or half days to nourish ourselves, to replenish our cup. A day out by the sea or in the forest, on your own for self-contemplation or with close friends who can listen and support you.

Taking longer walks in Nature, develops a deeper connection with Mother Nature. Notice how she changes with the season, admire her cyclical nature, and reflect on how she is a mirror to your own true wild nature. Sit and contemplate. Walk slowly, stop and smell the earth, let her fill your nostrils and expand your heart, pause and stand or hug a tree that calls you. Slow down and be in communion with the Great Mother. Let her hold you steady. She loves you unconditionally, nothing is too much for her to handle. Rest a while and feel her love embrace you.

I share more about connecting with our Sacred Trees in the chapter *Earth's Magical Gifts*.

Cold Water Swimming

To be honest I am generally a fair-weather swimmer. I tend to swim in the sea when the temperature starts to warm up in April. It's a wonderful way to fully cleanse and feel her soft silky waters against my skin.

I admire some of my friends who love to swim whatever the weather. Cold water has many health benefits and increasingly more people are taking the plunge.

Having said I don't like cold water, I do love to plunge into the icy waters of the White Spring, in Glastonbury, UK, the Isle of Avalon, the sacred heart of the planet, where the natural waters of the White Spring emerge from under the Tor into a dark cavern, lit with soft candlelight. It's a magical space with sacred altars dedicated to the goddesses and gods. It draws many people looking for spiritual connection, a peaceful place where in the echoes of the chamber song and chants vibrate around, creating a soft alluring sound bath. One of my greatest joys is taking women on annual retreat to Glastonbury. I book private access to the White Spring where I invite us to plunge into one of the icy pools for initiation and rebirth in the cleansing waters. Always a powerful and rejuvenating experience.

Sisterhood and the Power of Community

Being with like-minded friends is uplifting and empowering. We need like-minded soul sisters who are on a similar journey to us. Going on this journey will change you for the better and you need to surround yourself with positive friends and the environment where you can flourish.

Over time as you change, there will be times when you outgrow old relationships. This isn't a bad thing, although it can feel unsettling at the time, it is a natural thing. People come into our lives for a season and some for a lifetime, all have their purpose and gifts to share. Some challenge us to grow and elevate our energy and Light.

I invite you to honour your energy. Those that pull you down, who are jealous or envious of you, who you come away feeling drained rather than uplifted with, ask yourself the question whether it is time to move on. You will soon attract those people that are supportive and who value you deeply. It starts with valuing yourself first.

Some useful questions to reflect on are:

Does the person in question make you feel good inside and expansive or do you contract and want to pull away?

What people around you do you feel most comfortable with who get you, bring out the joy and light in you and cheer you on?

Are you ready to value yourself highly and move on?

Now is the time to invest in your self-care, so that you fill your cup up first.

Here are some tools I have personally used myself and with other women to guide us gently back to a nurturing relationship with our self. Self-love and self-acceptance are key for healing our wounding and addictive patterns of behaviour.

Daily Feminine Embodiment Practices

Return to these Feminine embodiment exercises throughout Winter so that they become the foundation of a new and continued personal practice.

You can also find free and paid Resources on my website that offer guided meditations and practices similar to the ones below. They are particularly helpful if you are someone who prefers to listen and be guided.

Womb Breathing

Take a luxurious 20-30 minutes per day

Take a deep breath down into your womb space and your own sacred cave.

Feel what you feel and without judgement allow your senses to become attuned to her vibration.

Trace your breath first around your hips creating a sense of your own sacred pelvic bowl.

Start with the inside of your right hip, tracing the breath down under your perineum and yoni and up the other side to the inside your left hip.

Return the breath back to your yoni, tracing up the centre line to your navel and belly button and back down and up your lower back from your coccyx (your tail bone) to the middle of your back, behind your belly button.

As you return to your womb, feel the breath expand into her space, breathing into the tight corners and the tightness in your hips.

If you experience pain, be gentle and embrace the pain with your breath. Allow any emotions that may be there to be felt and received by your heart. Allow any anger, sadness, shame and fear to rise. These are not to be feared but welcome them, so you can hold them in your loving heart.

You are making a reconnection with your womb, and she may well have lots to share and say to you, on an energetic and physical level.

There may be attachments to old relationships that still reside here that need honouring, forgiving, and letting go.

Make a note of your experiences as you explore and reconnect with this potent area of your body.

To do deep healing often needs someone skilled and experienced to hold the space for you to help you see through the noise with greater clarity. I have free and paid Resources on my website that offer Guided Meditations that you may wish to explore. Links can be found at the back of the book under Resources and About the Author.

Grounding

We often feel unbalanced when we are ungrounded. When feeling ungrounded we are not in our body and are not connected to our beautiful Earth.

Symptoms of feeling ungrounded:

Lightheaded and floaty

Mind and vision feel fuzzy.

Difficulty focussing

Disconnected from our feelings and emotions

Feel off balance

Bumping into things

Easily fall

Lack of physical energy and vitality

Grounding Meditation

Focusing your breath into your womb and belly. Then take your breath down your legs into your feet and toes.

Plant your feet firmly on the ground. Breathe out into the ground beneath you.

Imagine you have strong roots growing out from your hips and the souls of your feet (imagine a strong Oak or Beech tree and their roots) that go deep into the Earth beneath you.

Feel and visualise your roots following the roots of the tree, moving deeper and deeper through the structures of the inner Earth, following the flows of the underground rivers and streams.

Intend that your roots go deep into the Heart of Mother Earth, Gaia and her diamond light centre and emerald, green heart. Anchor your roots here and allow Mother Earth to hold and love you. Rest here a few minutes in her peaceful heart.

When you are ready, breathe her life force up your roots, as if you are drinking her sap to replenish your body. Feel her move through your veins, blood, and bones, strengthening them, breathing her deep into your womb and belly to energise and replenish. And then up into your heart. Feel her love.

Allow your heart to open and soften, expanding your capacity to receive as well as give. As your heart expands, your crown at the top of your head begins to gradually open to reveal a beautiful lotus flower.

Feel your connection with the Moon, the Sun, and the Stars in the Cosmos.

Breathe in the starlight and let it fall into your heart.

Breathe, relax, and let go.

Sit and bathe in these energies until you feel balanced and replenished.

You may wish to listen to my Guided Meditation 'Connect and Ground'. The Link can be found at the back of the book under Resources.

Self-massage

Touch and massage are a wonderful way to come back into the body.

One of the simple things you can introduce into your bathing ritual is a beautiful, nourishing massage. Use natural products that nourish your belly and breasts. Such as: Coconut oil, essential oils, avocado base oil, Almond base oil. I love to use essential oils of calendula, rose or lavender, just one or two drops to some base oil to add a fragrance to enhance my senses and help me relax. These oils are very nourishing for the skin but always check with a qualified aromatherapist to see what they recommend. Always test a small area of your skin first before putting over your whole body to make sure you are not overly sensitive or allergic to any of the oils.

Extend your bath or shower time to include a gentle circular massage over and around your belly in clockwise directions. It will start to connect you with your womb centre and brings your attention out of your head back to your body. Feel the sensual curves of your body, belly, and hips, enjoying the simple pleasure of soft touch. Caress her and thank her for her beauty.

You might like to also experiment with playful curiosity your vulva or yoni as I love to call her. Yoni is a sacred name for our vulva and vagina. She is considered the mouth of the Goddess and gateway to our womb. Connecting with our yoni using oils that are safe in this delicate and highly sensitised area such as Coconut Oil or Yoni Sacred oil. Notice what touch and strokes create pleasure in your body. We have been told so many negative thoughts about our body as being a sexual commodity that can be bought or manipulated. Some of us have suffered physical and emotional abuse that has naturally created shock and withdrawal in the body. Through our gentle touch we can bring her home to a place of safety in our hearts, learning what feels good to her, taking back our power. We are designed to receive and give pleasure.

I remember thinking as a child that exploring my vulva and vagina and pleasuring myself was a dirty thing to be hidden rather than celebrated. We have a lot of layers to de armour, to unravel all the shame and conditioning. We can begin this healing process with gentle touch, self-awareness and honouring our She temple by listening and respecting her wishes. Then we become confident to express her needs and desires. Holding clear boundaries is important for you to learn to trust and feel safe in your body. This is where deep womb and sexual healing is really needed at this time of feminine awakening and empowerment for our sexual power is fundamental to our power as women.

If you are in a loving partnership, you could invite your partner to participate in gentle touch and massage. Opening ourselves to another creates a space of intimacy and potential vulnerability so only do this if you feel safe and are ready to trust your partner. Create clear boundaries around what you want, what you like and dislike. Invite a playful attitude, one that is nourishing rather than sexual at this stage.

We go into depth with our feminine sexuality and sensuality in my Spring/Summer Book and all the issues we are unravelling to fully awaken and embody our passionate life force.

Energy Cleansing Bath

To cleanse your energy is especially beneficial if you feel you have taken on or absorbed negativity from others' energies. It can also be if you have felt overstimulated and you want to calm your energy and nervous system and ground. It's a great daily practice to get into, as the more you clear your energy the higher you will be able to hold your vibration and attract more of what you desire.

Also, when you develop a regular routine, your antennae becomes much sharper and so you soon become aware of when you are out of balance and when you need to protect your energies from others. Media and the news are common triggers for people; we can come away feeling drained, or unconsciously taking on others' emotions and feelings.

There are a few ways you can cleanse your energy.

White Light

Create a space where you will feel comfortable, and you won't be disturbed.

Cleanse your energy with White Light, imagining it is coming in through the crown and top of your head. You can also call upon the Violet Flame which is the Universal Ray of transmutation governed by Lord St Germain, one of the Ascended Masters who supports humanity in raising our vibration.

Feel and see your body bathed in Light.

Visualise each of your energy centres (the seven major chakras: crown, third eye, throat, heart, solar plexus/navel, sacral and root) being filled and cleansed with the Light.

Allow these energies to flow into the Earth, asking the Earth to transmute any heavy energy, that may have become attached to you during the day or that you accidentally absorbed from others.

You may see colours or feel sensations in your body as you are having an 'energetic cleanse' and wash.

Filling up with Light

Once your cleansing feels complete, we must fill ourselves up with positive life enhancing energy.

Allow a colour or rainbow colours to flow down over you, bathing and replenishing you. You could use white, gold, yellow, green, blue whatever colour you feel you need or surrender and allow your Higher Self to bring you what you need.

Bathe in these energies until you feel full of Light, making sure you are grounding and sending your roots into the heart of Mother Earth (see my Grounding Meditation).

Smudging with Sacred Herbs

White Sage and **Palo Santo** wood sticks are ones I use regularly. They are both excellent for cleansing energy. If you are buying them, it is worth checking they are grown and harvested in sustainable ways that honours the sacredness of the tree. You can also make your own sage stick from wild sage grown in the garden combined with perhaps lavender and rosemary both of which are healing and purifying. Remember when you are taking anything from the Earth, you give something in return, a gift of love, as song, a prayer and traditionally in indigenous countries they would have offered tobacco to the spirits in gratitude.

White Sage has been used for centuries by the Native Americans to purify and ward off negative spirits and energy. It is more pungent and is great for purifying and clearing space as well. They come either as an incense stick bundle, tightly bound, or loose leaf.

To begin your cleansing, come to your heart and offer to the spirit your prayers and intentions with gratitude.

Light the stick or the end of the leaf and then fan out the flame with your hand or a feather so that it begins to smoke. It is the smoke that you use to waft around your body and aura. Either use your hands or if you have one, use a feather to fan the smoke towards your body. The feather represents the elements Air and Spirit, so again thanking the spirits for blowing away negativity and bringing in the sacredness of spirit.

Work from top to bottom, front and back, hands and feet, bringing the smoke to the chakras as you work down the front and spine of the body. It is great at clearing heavy energy and excess energy you may have accumulated.

I use this at the beginning of my shamanic women's circles and when I work individually.

Palo Santo is sold as small batons of wood that have fallen from the Palo Santo tree found in Peru, Ecuador, and other South American countries. It grows in dry tropical forests and produces fragrant resin. It is part of the same family (Burseraceae) as frankincense and myrrh. In Spanish, Palo Santo means 'holy wood.'

Palo Santo has a sweet aroma and doesn't smoke like white sage. It brings in positivity and has a calming effect on the heart and mind.

Again, light it at the end of the stick and fan the small flame so it gently sends small spirals of smoke up into the air. You can hold the wood and gradually work round the crown of your head and down the body in the same way, affirming your prayers for what you wish to receive more of in your life.

Palo Santo is also great to carry safely in your pocket if you are out in Nature and want to light it and honour a tree or sacred site with its sacred scent.

Clear Boundaries Practice

Having cleansed your energy, you are now ready to focus on your energetic boundaries.

Our boundaries create safety.

As you scan your energy and body, imagine you can see or sense where your aura finishes around you. Is it close to your body or further away from you?

Quite often under stress or when we are in fear, our energy naturally contracts inwards as we withdraw our energies from places, spaces, and people we don't feel comfortable with. What is more beneficial is to expand our aura and make it strong so that our energy can withstand other energies rather than succumb to them.

When our aura is weak, and we are ungrounded, we are more susceptible to the influence of other energies. Our immune system is compromised too.

Using your breath, visualise your energy expanding to a comfortable two metres distance all around you for everyday situations – in front of you, beneath you, to the sides of you, front and back. Feel like you are expanding the 'egg' shape of your aura around you.

Expand even further if this feels comfortable, filling the room with your presence and Light.

With your breath again invite a strong colour or symbol. Such as:

Violet or dark blue for protection

Green for balance and healing

Gold for strength and vibrancy

Pink for Love

Symbols

The symbol of the **Solar Cross** in a circle is also a powerful balancing symbol that you can place visually in your aura.

The Flower of Life geometric symbol shows the beauty of creation with its interlocking petal flowers. It exists as a Divine blueprint within each plant, flower, tree, shell. I wear a Flower of Life pendant and visualise this placed over and within my aura to create balance, infinite potential, and creativity.

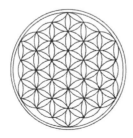

Using colour and/or a symbol combined with grounding your roots into the Earth, like a tree helps to strengthen our energy that nourishes the physical body and keeps our emotions calm and centred.

If there is a particular person you are finding it difficult to be with and wish to have more detachment from, you can use the **Infinity Symbol**, (figure of eight).

Place yourself within one circle and the other person in the other circle of the symbol.

Visualise a bright blue energy flowing in the shape of the Infinity Symbol. This creates distance and detachment from their energy.

Spend a few minutes visualising and feeling the strength of the **Infinity Symbol** creating more separation between the two of you whilst feeling connected in Love.

Mind, Body and Soul Nourishment

Let's look at the three levels we want to feel nourished.

When we create positive intentions for each of the following areas, we recognise their value and the difference they can have on our quality of life.

Exercise

Take an A4 piece of paper and draw a line down the middle making sure there is room to write on either side.

Make the left column your negative thoughts and the right column your new positive thoughts.

Write down all the negative thoughts and chatter you tell yourself or have been told. Become aware whose voice is speaking.

Then take your time to check with your heart.

Is this truth speaking?

Whose voice is it speaking?

Quite often we take on others' beliefs and thoughts that were spoken when we were children. Or we may have created beliefs after a horrible experience that has shut us down to the potential to receive more love and abundance.

Use the following ideas to create new positive thoughts and beliefs that you can write in your right-hand column.

Start with....

I am.......

I choose......

I allow......

I am open to ....

Choose one or two to become your daily mantra. Place sticky notes on your mirror or fridge to remind you each morning.

Here are some examples to help you.

Mind
Intention:

I am peaceful, calm, and clear. I hold positive and loving thoughts and beliefs about myself.

I trust I am ENOUGH just as I am. I am perfect. I love and accept myself unconditionally.

Body
Intention:

I feel relaxed and soft, I nourish my beautiful body on the inside and outside.

I am perfect as I am.

I am desirable.

**Soul
Intention:**

I am inspired, loving and compassionate towards myself and others.

Creative Winter Projects

Work with clay as a medium of the Earth. It is very therapeutic, helping to quieten the mind and come back into the body. Mould your clay after being out in Nature or a cold winter's day next to a warm fire. Allow your hands to mould, going with the flow. Or you may wish to make the clay into a pot or womb shape.

Writing a description of how you feel about Winter, perhaps a poem or form of prose.

Wood

On a walk-in Nature, choose a piece of wood from one of the sacred trees that calls you. Always remember to honour them with respect and gratitude.

You could take a piece of wood that has fallen, using it as a symbol of what you are letting go. Equally, it is a great way to connect with the essence and spirit of the tree, noticing how the wood feels. Work with the wood to plane it down, to perhaps shape it into a Wand or a Talking Stick. I share more about the sacred trees I have been called to work with under the chapter 5: *Earth's Magical Gifts and Sacred Trees.*

Your Commitment to Self-Care

Journal Prompts

Let us look at bringing some focus to your day.

How can you bring more self-nourishment into your life?

Where can you create more space for 'Me' time?

Taking little steps is the place to start.

What self-nourishment can you bring into your life today?

What would be most beneficial for you today?

What would you be prepared to commit to this week?

Remember this is a commitment to yourself; no-one else.

What can you delegate to your family or externally if it is related to work or housework?

Where do you need to say NO to other people's demands or negotiate so you have more space for you?

Think of your boundaries here and where they may need firming up. Do you feel confident to voice your truth? Low self-esteem and self-worth can affect our ability to speak up and stand up for our needs. Doing the regular cleansing and self-care practices will start to help you become clearer. The more you value and give to yourself, the stronger you will become.

Resisiance io Change

How to Handle Self-sabotage

Let's get real, we all find change difficult and uncomfortable at times. With ingrained habits and behaviours, resistance can surface that makes it difficult to make the changes in lifestyle that we really know deep down would be beneficial for us.

Why does this happen when we want change so badly?

Guilt may surface, "What will people think of me if I spend time on myself? What will happen if I change? Will I still be loved? Will my friends and partner disown me? Will my friends desert me? Will they judge me?" The list goes on. We distract ourselves with clearing up instead, watching endless TV and Netflix, binging on chocolate biscuits and crisps. Let's be honest, none of these are going to help raise our vibration and get us moving towards our dream reality. Not to say some of this isn't lovely some of the time, but are you avoiding what you truly want?

It's time to listen to your inner needs and desires, your wild wise woman that's calling you.

If you find it increasingly difficult to create time for relaxation and you always keep finding yourself in the same loop of behaviour giving and helping others, take some time to answer these questions honestly of yourself:

- Trace back and look at how you behaved as a child. Did you feel the need to adapt your behaviour, to feel loved?

- Were you loved unconditionally, or was love given conditionally dependent on your good behaviour? Good girl vs bad girl!
- What stops you having time for yourself?
- What feelings and emotions come up when you consider having 'me' time?
- Do you feel guilty for putting your needs before others?
- What was your mother's attitude to her own self-care?
- What influence did your father have on your mother and the family?

When we are growing up, it is easy to take on what we perceive as acceptable behaviour from our parents and siblings.

Many of us feel guilty for spending time on ourselves, feeling it is indulgent and selfish. However, if we harbour feelings of resentment because our needs aren't getting met and there isn't balance in a relationship, this can be very damaging to our long-term health and wellbeing.

Be absolutely honest with yourself about your underlying motives. We all have them. Sometimes there is something to be gained by adopting the continuous pattern or behaviour. We call these 'secondary benefits.' Often, they lie hidden under the surface in the unconscious.

For example, if I continue to give, then I feel needed and wanted, therefore satisfying some inner need for validation and approval. You may continue the behaviour in the hope that others may respond and care for you or give something in return. This becomes a co-dependent relationship.

This is usually an unconscious pattern and can be difficult to break on your own.

However, once you decide you are ready to create a more loving and respectful relationship with yourself, you can find ways to break free. Seeking help from a professional to help create that energetic shift and breakthrough can be life-changing. Decide to love yourself anyway and begin what we call the re-parenting process of mothering and nurturing yourself and your inner child.

Healing Our Wombs

So often we find emotions and trauma lie in the shadows of the womb that keep us from truly living from a place of joy and empowerment.

We may hold fear, guilt, shame, physical and emotional trauma due to physical, sexual and emotional abuse.

One of the tell-tale signs of a disconnection with our womb power is poor boundaries we have in relationship to our family, friends, partner and previous partners that may still have an energetic imprint on our womb energy and space.

Situations and challenges arise for us to go deeper into our healing journey. People can trigger old emotions and old relationships may re-enter our life to enable some form of resolution and completion. This is a time to pause and feel what is still present and discover what is the root cause of our disharmony. It is usually a sign that we have given our power away and it is time to reclaim our power and life force, through love and forgiveness.

Winter is the perfect time to go deeper to explore our inner healing so that we rise rooted, as an empowered joyful Woman.

Building a deeper connection with our womb and a developing a daily practice will aid our healing. Let us remember the joy and pleasure that our womb was created for.

Ancestral Patterning

Often our patterning and limitations relate to our upbringing and social conditioning. What we perceived was allowable or acceptable behaviour then, sets up a belief pattern and associated feelings and emotions that then run the show.

In my own life I was the youngest of three daughters. My sisters were well meaning in their attempts to know what was best for me. And yet being the youngest, I felt I was having to follow their way, and so I felt I couldn't fully express my own needs and desires which contributed to self-doubt. I was acutely sensitive, shy, and never felt good enough. I held on to my emotions as I didn't feel safe to express how I felt, feeling there were unspoken expectations of having to be more mature than I was. Our mother and father were always busy working and had limited time except for holidays to play with us. Being sensitive I lacked the affection and tangible support that I felt I truly needed for me to flourish. These conditions undermined my level of self-esteem and self-worth. This created a lot of tension and insecurity in my body. This is not to say that love did not exist in our family because it did and does to this day. As I have healed, forgiven and let go, I recognise the way I need to receive love is different to the way they were able to give it. It has been a long journey of unravelling these patterns and I continue to do so along the different levels of the healing spiral, allowing my true authentic self to emerge.

We also experience many patterns and beliefs that have been passed on down our mother and father line, what we refer to as ancestral patterning that comes down through our DNA and umbilical cord. In my mother line, I recognise the women had great difficulty expressing their needs and truth and that our mother never had the affection she needed from her parents. It is a generational thing that gets passed down the line.

It doesn't mean that we can't change the beliefs, patterns and traumas that have been passed down. Nothing is written in stone what is to become. We can interrupt and break the chain so that we become free, also freeing the past for all and for the benefit of our future generations, as we are all connected in the web of life. As this has been my journey to heal my ancestral lineage, I have become adept and skilled at helping and supporting others to break free of the chains that bind.

As we journey through Winter, you will discover Her wisdom and the alchemical power of the Womb, allowing you to increasingly free yourself from past conditioning. In Part Two, we focus on Facing our Shadows and Ancestral Healing.

Past Lives

I believe we exist within circular time and that we have experienced many lives and roles incarnate as a woman and man. Before we come into our current life, our Soul's agree the kind of life that we wish to lead, one that helps the soul grow and evolve. We have this opportunity to make good past mistakes and reap the lessons and balance the law of Karma – the Universal Law of Cause and Effect – this is where the saying, 'We reap what we sow,' comes from.

My soul journey, is for example, to reclaim my authentic power as a woman, to live in full alignment with my soul and higher purpose and in doing so help other women to do the same. Within this there are many lessons and core wounds I have had to heal such as the wound of judgement and betrayal. Many of life's challenges and lessons have helped me explore, heal, and transform these earlier experiences and I go on to explore these further in Part Two, in chapter on Ancestral Healing. It's a continual process of growth and ascension, rising higher in my Love vibration so that I can forgive and accept myself and others, despite our differences. Ultimately my purpose is to assist the Earth at this time of great evolution and change to return to a place of unity consciousness where we are connected as One Tribe regardless of gender, preference, religion, race, creed, or colour.

How is the past affecting you now?

What threads can you see flowing through your lineage to how you live your current life?

What are you ready to break free from?

Journal Prompts - Self-Nourishment

What does self-nourishment feel and look like to you?

Is it a relaxing bath with scented oils, candles, and relaxing music?

Is it a gentle walk in Nature or perhaps dancing and moving to your favourite music?

Is it treating yourself to beautiful colours in your bedroom that make you feel nourished on a soul and emotional level?

Quiet relaxation, reflection and allowing space to contemplate and daydream is another way to lose yourself in the moment.

Write in Your Journal.

How would you like to feel nourished?

What would you like more of or less of in your life?

Nourishing food

How does your diet mirror how much you love and value yourself?

Are there things you can cut out or introduce to bring balance?

Incorporate Winter's root vegetables in your diet to help you feel grounded and nourished. Include warming soups and hearty stews to bring comfort during the cold dark months of the year. Bring the warming colours of orange for the sacral chakra and red say from beetroot, sweet potato, and red cabbage to help you ground and earth.

We are what we eat. Nutritious wholesome food is a wonderful way to feel good and nourished on all levels. It really does light us up from the inside out.

CHAPTER 9.
Creating Sacred Space and Sacred Ceremony

Creating our own sacred space is a beautiful way to support ourselves on the journey. It brings into form that which delights our heart and soothes our soul, giving us a physical reminder of the season and lunar cycle, we are currently in.

It gives space for prayer and contemplation, for rest and meditation and for sharing our gratitude to Mother Earth and the benevolent Universal forces that support our life's path. It can be a physical reminder of what we want to attract more of into our lives, thereby magnifying our heart desires.

I make reference to simple rituals and ceremonies in Part Two so I would like to offer ways for you to create your own sacred space, rituals and ceremonies and some of the magical ingredients that can make it a beautiful and meaningful experience.

Where to Create Sacred Space?

You can set up your sacred space practically anywhere. You can have it in your own home, in a corner of a bedroom, a small table in your lounge or perhaps you have a room in the garden that is dedicated to relaxation that would be suitable.

Imagine for a moment a beautiful light-filled space that would encourage you to keep coming back to nurture yourself and your spiritual and earthly connection.

What would it look and feel like?

What colours or qualities are important to you?

Are there things you have collected on your Nature walks and travels that you wish to have on show, that hold special meaning for you?

Inside Sacred Space

In our own home, I have two small tables, one draped with a blue silk cloth, the other bare wood and simple. In the centre of the first one, I have a decorated bowl of sacred blessed water, representing our womb chalice, the container for our sacred water that offers new life and renewal.

I honour all the five elements:

For **Fire**: I burn a candle, sometimes three candles, representing the Divine Feminine, the Divine Masculine and our Divine Child.

For **Air** I display a beautiful peacock feather that was gifted to me. Peacock is symbolic of the Divine Feminine in her magnificence. Any feather that falls on your path is a beautiful gift from spirit.

For **Earth**: I have beautiful crystals, such as Rose Quartz for unconditional Love and Carnelian, a beautiful orange stone which is good for awakening our Sacral creative energies in our pelvic bowl.

For **Water**: I have a small bowl or chalice that holds sacred blessed water. This could be local spring water. For me, I use the Chalice Well waters of the Red and White Spring, found in Glastonbury, Somerset, UK.

For Great Spirit/Creator: I have a round, wooden sphere made in the sacred geometric symbol of the Flower of Life. This represents the seed of creation, what we discovered in the *Spiral of Life* in Part One.

I love to have fresh seasonal flowers, usually roses representing our sacred Rose Heart, symbolic of the Divine Feminine and the Rose Lineage through the ages. Winter's natural foliage, such as Holly and bare twigs and wood is symbolic of Winter medicine.

Finally, I have a small stone statue of the Goddess, handmade and bought at Avebury, Wiltshire in the UK, an ancient sacred Stone Circle, known for being a powerful portal for the Earth, the Divine Feminine and our connection to the star constellations.

On my other table, amongst other things, I have a statue that was gifted to me, representing the union of the Divine Feminine and Divine Masculine.

I also like to add Oracle cards I have chosen for each Lunar cycle, to give focus and increase my self-awareness of what is transcending and awakening within me.

At each turn of the Wheel of the Year, I feel the urge to wipe clear my sacred space and create anew. Often, I use the same items of significance and meaning, but bring new and fresh flowers, foliage and colours, choosing new crystals and intentions. In my creative phases, I will add my own drawings and paintings to the sacred space, so sometimes the space can become rather full.

Outside Sacred Space

If you have the pleasure of your own garden or communal garden, you may like to create a special place that reflects the changing seasons. For me I have a special place that I have created at the base of our Apple Tree that I use for ritual and ceremony. A stone statue of a small Buddha sits within the long grass that has grown around the trunk, representing peace and stillness. Colourful crystals, stones, and shells that I have collected on my walks also get placed here.

You will often find me there lighting a candle, giving thanks, leaving sweet offerings to the Elemental Beings and Nature Spirits in gratitude. I especially love to do this around the Full Moon and at the Equinox and Solstices, as the Earth energies are most potent then. It is a great time to align with the energies, to come into rightful balance and to honour all that is manifesting.

Letting Go

In times of letting go, I burn old papers and notes of what I want to release in my little cauldron, often at the Full Moon.

When I am going through deep healing and transformation, I like to bring items from Nature that represent what I wish to let go of, such as broken or rotting sticks, tree branches, large stones, dried flowers. I found this especially helpful, when I was healing my father's ancestral lineage and found a rotting stick which was symbolic of what was ready to go. In this case I buried the stick with intention, and I share more of this story in Part Two under *Ancestral Healing*.

Equally, flowers or seeds that I have grown can be an active way of planting new hopes and dreams in the fertile Earth. I feel such joy and excitement when I first see green shoots in Spring – it is a beautiful way to heal and grow a deeper loving connection with our Earth Mother.

Overleaf I share the overall process for setting up and creating ceremony.

Creating Magical Ceremony

When I was thinking about writing this next section, I found myself reflecting on the beautiful ceremonies and rituals I have created with many groups of women and on my own. I found that there were some important ingredients that really contributed to creating a beautiful and meaningful ceremony. I want to share these little secrets with you so you can create something simple yet remarkable too.

Five Secrets for Creating Your Own Magical Ceremony:

1. Connecting with your childlike **wonder** and **magic**
2. Clear **intention** and prayer
3. **Non-attachment – Letting go of expectations**
4. A **grateful** and open heart
5. Keep it **simple**, follow your own heart's **truth**.

1. Magic of Ceremony

From when I was a small innocent child I believed in a magical world and the mysteries of the Universe. It was a palpable feeling that I could feel inside my heart - the intrinsic design and web of the Universe that I was a part of.

I remember the childlike wonder of blowing out my birthday candles having made a wish. Watching the smoke whirl round and dance up into the air and that inner knowing and belief that somehow my wishes would be granted just by magic!

Can you remember a time when you felt the magic and innocence of your childhood?

*Take a moment to **breathe and expand the feeling**.*

*What would the magical child inside you want to **create**?*

We can create that same feeling when we enter the space of Ceremony.

That is the power and magic of ceremony.

2. Clear Intentions and Prayer

A ceremony or ritual involves the simple act of focusing our energy and motivation behind our prayers and intentions. When we declare our intent and call on the power of the Universe, it goes into action to make manifest that which we desire.

It could simply be lighting a candle and blowing it out with intent, just like we did as a child.

It helps to be clear of our intentions. Writing them down helps to ground them, although you may prefer to be spontaneous. Speaking our prayers out loud gives them power, not only to ourselves but if we are doing it with others, to be witnessed, it is equally healing and empowering.

3. Non-attachment – Let Go of Expectations

Usually, the creative outcome of our prayers and intentions manifests when we least expect.

- Have you ever experienced a time when you have been so desperate for something to happen that somehow you knew you were blocking the outcome?
- Why is this?

This is because we have become too attached to a specific outcome.

When we enter a state of non-attachment, letting go of expectations of how and when it will come about, then the Universal energies can flow unhindered. The Universe will answer either directly through personal experience or through events, people, and situations, in tangible and non-tangible ways and with magical synchronicity.

The **key** is to be open, to receive and to let go of any attachments of how, when and where it will happen. Declare your intention and then let the Universe work out the 'how.'

For example: -

I was listening to one of my favourite *Cold Play*'s songs. Whilst dancing around the kitchen in joy, I said out loud: "I would love to see them live in concert." Without thinking much more about it, a couple of hours later I was checking my messages and I had received an invitation from a friend to join her to see them live in a few weeks' time. You can imagine my surprise and delight.

It doesn't always happen that quickly. The important thing is to remain in a state of trust and openness, knowing that the perfect time will come.

My sacred prayer always finishes with - "for the highest good and the most benevolent outcome". This allows the Universe to bring me the best possible outcome without harm to anyone else.

4. Fostering a Grateful Heart

When we experience deep gratitude and accept the simplest of things as little miracles, we raise our vibration and return to a place of love and peace with all things.

Giving thanks and being appreciative helps us to receive more of the same. It creates space for more positive to come into our life.

The Universal Law of Attraction works on the basis that 'like attracts like' so feeling grateful naturally attracts more abundance into our life. We become a magnet to our own desires.

Coming from a place of gratitude, as if our prayers and intentions have already been given, is a wonderful way to enter and begin our ceremony.

Reflect upon all the things you are grateful for in Nature – her beauty and abundance and how she has supported you through each season.

Consider your friends and family who support you, love you and care for you, and show up when you most need them.

Be grateful for yourself – focus on your strengths, your gifts, and the wisdom you have gained through life's challenges.

Writing a **gratitude journal** teaches our subconscious mind to focus on the positive things to be grateful for – even on bad days.

5. Simplicity

Follow your heart, create what's right for you, adapt it so it is meaningful for you. You don't have to create something complex. Simple is beautiful.

Five Steps to Creating Sacred Ceremony

1. Getting Started

Firstly, contemplate the following questions so you are clear why you want to create ceremony?

- What is your intention for this ceremony?
- What do you want to create more of in your life?
- What do you want to release and let go of?
- Is this a ceremony on your own or with others?

Gather the materials you would like to have, that create beauty, simplicity, love and are symbolic of what you desire and wish to let go of.

2. Laying Out Your Circle

When we are creating ceremonial space we may want to work with a circle, as this is representative of the circle of life where all things flow continuously.

To represent the **Five Elements**, decide where East, West, North, South is and mark these out with candles or stones. If you are unsure, you can work with the 'magical compass' ie, choosing where you want them to be and using your intention to mark the spot.

Mark the **centre** with a candle or ring of candles, crystals, flowers, and anything else of meaning. The centre is the focus of your ceremony and wishes.

3. Opening Sacred Space

First, call in the Four Directions – the elements of Earth (North), Air (East), Fire (South), Water (West), lighting your candles in turn. Speak these out loud to bring power.

Welcome each element with an open heart asking for their blessings and healing for your ceremony.

You are calling them in to help assist you. They are powerful and magical, so they deserve respect.

For example:

"I call upon the **Power of Fire** – to bring me light and warmth, to alchemise and transform, to awaken my inner passion and the fire in my heart. Aho (thank you, thank you, thank you)." In Shamanic traditions "Aho" is used to give thanks at the end of a prayer."I call upon the **Power of Water** – the eternal waters of life, to cleanse and bring flow, so that I/we may give birth to new beginnings. Aho (thank you, thank you, thank you)."

"I call upon the **Power of Earth** – to bring stability and to help me build strong foundations, to help me learn from your natural ways. I honour the Ancestors who have gone before me and call upon their wisdom and guidance that I may follow a path of truth. Aho (thank you, thank you, thank you)." "I call upon the **Power of Air** – to help me see the bigger picture, to bring me clarity, to blow away the old and renew me with fresh prana. To help me speak my truth from the heart. Aho (thank you, thank you, thank you)."

If you have a drum or rattle, you may like to honour each Direction with a beat of the drum or shake of the rattle.

For the **Centre**:

"I call upon Mother Earth to support me so that I may learn your wisdom to live in balance and harmony. I honour all the kingdoms as One – the two legged, the four legged, the finned, the furred and the winged ones. Aho (thank you, thank you, thank you)

"I call upon the Father Sun, Father Sky, Grandmother Moon, the Star Nations. Aho (thank you, thank you, thank you)."

When you've called in the Four Directions, as above, you can settle yourself comfortably to begin the main part of the ritual.

In the centre, now declare your intentions for the ceremony ie

I ask for your Universal guidance and healing for help with ....

I wish to release....

I wish to attract more of ....

Please show me the way to ....

Please help me to align with my higher purpose...

A prayer for the world....

You may also make a wish on behalf of someone else who you know needs healing and support. It is of course, their free choice how they wish to experience their life, but you may send them positive prayers and energy to support them through any difficulty or to just wish them well on their life's path.

4. The Ceremony

Sit quietly, to receive guidance, then follow your intuition.

Do you need to burn old papers or a note of what you wish to release?

Do you want to read out a poem?

Declare your dreams and wishes – speak them out loud with passion and conviction.

5. Closing Sacred Space/Ceremony

Give thanks and gratitude to the elements, to your spirit guides and to the consciousness of Mother Earth, Gaia, and Father Sun/Sky and all the beings that you have called in.

You can give thanks by saying something like:

"**Power of Fire**, I honour and thank you for your blessings and bid you farewell. Aho."

Repeat this for each powerful element.

Feel the energies gradually move away knowing they have left a positive imprint in the land and on your heart.

Blow out any candles, leaving the space safe for others to find.

You may like to leave any offerings such as flowers to die naturally and return to the Earth, taking your wishes with you.

Note any insights in your journal.

Sacred Cacao Plant Medicine

Cacao is a sacred plant medicine of Mother Earth and as I described earlier is a beautiful healing medicine that safely and gently opens the heart and boosts the immune system. It has so many amazing benefits that I have included it under *Earth's Magical Gifts*.

You can use Mamma Cacao to enhance your sacred ceremony, to open the heart and deepen your experience with Mother Earth and Spirit. It contains dopamine so induces a sense of pleasure and feeling good in oneself.

It is best to buy Ceremonial Cacao from a reputable and sustainable source and I share a couple under *Book Resources*.

There are a few contraindications, including people who take antidepressants, or have serious heart conditions, and if you are pregnant or breastfeeding you should reduce the amount you take as the cacao is stimulating. Please investigate these fully first or consult a doctor if you are unsure.

Preparation

Make up Cacao with milk or just water, grating the large raw cacao to the quantity that feels appropriate for you. Usually anything between 10-15g per 200g of milk is the daily dose or for ceremonial use you can increase the amount. If you buy Cacao in its raw bean state, you can grate it so it melts gently under a low heat making sure it doesn't boil as this will destroy the nutritional qualities. Follow the instructions that come with your Cacao.

Personally, I love to make mine with almond milk, but you can use oat milk, or any other vegan milk is suggested. You may like to sweeten it with a little honey or agave syrup if you find it too bitter. I also sometimes add a drop of sweet orange essential oil or rose otto essential oil, but this is not necessary.

The Power of Intention

Like we discussed earlier, having clear intentions is important before we enter sacred space.

Sankalpa is the **Sanskrit word for intention**. San means 'to become one with' and kalpa means 'time' and 'subconscious mind.'

Sankalpa

"What is my Soul's longing?"
A Sankalpa is a heartfelt intention reflecting our highest ideals.
The Sankalpa helps us focus and empower our deepest heart desires

Whilst you are preparing your Cacao medicine, it is important to honour the spirit of Mamma Cacao. Before making your cup of Cacao, you may like to place her in your sacred space, on a plate surrounded by flowers and rose petals, for a few hours. Infuse songs and prayers that express gratitude and your Sankalpa, giving thanks for her generous spirit. The energy of your intentions (Sankalpa) becomes part of the ingredients that make up the healing medicine of Mamma Cacao.

Here is a sacred song that you can invite into the ritual of making your cup of Cacao.

"Cacaocita, la medicina

Cacaocita, la di di di

Cacaocita, la medicina

Cacaocita, la di di di

Cura, cura cuerpecito,

Cura, cura, la di di di

Limpia, limpia, espiratito,

Limpia, limpia, la di di di

Words: Florencia Fridman – Cacao Lab

I have shared a YouTube song you may wish to listen to: Cacao Spirit Song. Link can be found at the back of the book under Resources.

Enjoy this beautiful heart opening medicine on your own or with others in celebration of your spirit and the spirit in all things.

Sacred Heart Offerings

Walking a path of beauty is to honour and respect all life. Where you connect with a tree that calls you or you spend time in a sacred site, always leave your appreciation and thanks with a sacred offering. You can use flowers, herbs, something you have made from natural material, stones and crystals imbued with your love and prayers, spring water that you have blessed. A tree may benefit from burning white sage or Palo Santo. Tune in and see what you feel called to offer, always honouring all life with respect.

As we walk the Earth and connect deeper to her rhythms, we may notice the playful influence of the Nature Spirits all around us, in the wind, in the dancing raindrops, in the warming sunrays and the heartbeat of the Earth herself, beneath our feet. She arouses our playful spirit, the young innocent Maiden within, that part of us that is full of wonder and curiosity.

There is a simplicity and way of being that we have lost as human beings and I know that the more we wake from our 'sleep' and open our hearts, we will remember the power and sacredness of living in harmony with the Earth and all sentient beings. There is hope and peace that we can align to if we choose to focus our energies and attention here.

Magical Synchronicities – Your Dreams are on Their Way!

Look out for Universal signs that your dream, your wish, is on its way.

Universal signs are there all the time guiding us along our path.

You may find you turn to a book and read a sentence that stands out or hear the words of a song that really resonate with you.

It could be a friend calls you or you bump into someone unexpectedly that says something that guides you to another person or place.

The signs are always there in Nature, something She leaves on your path, a bird song, a butterfly, a rainbow.

The Universe is a benevolent force that wants us to succeed and be happy.

It is our Divine birthright to be abundant and to live a purposeful and joyful life. The more we can hold a vision of what we want, yet surrender to how it will come to us, the easier we will find things and circumstances will naturally flow to us.

Sometimes we experience what we would call challenges that help us release blocks to receiving the full abundance of our dreams. This helps us grow and strengthen ready to receive and fully live our dreams.

The Universe knows the bigger picture of our lives and sometimes things occur in a different order to what we would imagine or desire but always, in my personal experience, in accordance with our highest wishes and for the greatest good of All.

Often, we can self-sabotage our dreams because at some unconscious level we hold limiting beliefs of unworthiness, of lack, of not enough. When we heal and release these patterns with love and forgiveness, we start to open to so many more possibilities.

You can create your own personal gratitude ceremony. Alternatively, you may like to join with others to collectively share in gratitude, making it an even more powerful experience.

I share '**How to Create a Gratitude Ceremony'** in my *Autumn Spiral* book, to give deep thanks for Nature's harvest and our personal 'inner harvest.' A Gratitude, or 'Despachio' Ceremony, that the ancient Inca people created to honour all life, is a deeply nourishing, loving and a humbling experience. It offers a beautiful way to invite the flow of fertility, abundance, wellness, good health, and prosperity in our life.

Journal Prompts

What in your life needs honouring and celebrating with ceremony?

How can you use sacred ceremony to help you let go and heal?

Who would you like to gather with you to create a sacred circle together?

Reflections

Beautiful Woman I see you

I believe in You.

We know the importance of connecting with our body and the Earth.

She is our solid foundation from which we build an authentic, aligned, peaceful and abundant life.

Take time to reflect on your connection to your body and the Earth.

How do you want to feel different in your life?

What commitment are you prepared to put into your self-care, self-nourishment, and personal healing?

What small step or steps can you begin with today?

Having given you a nourishing framework for our journey together, let's dive into the magic of Winter Wisdom.

PART TWO:

THE STORY OF WINTER

Winter's Invitation

All is within

Find yourself deep inside

The beauty of your inner Cave

Let Her hold you, nurture you

Allow you to Be

Rest and Dream

Who and what are you becoming?

***

In the darkness, we discover the answers to our worries and doubts

We find our inner Light, our inner Flame

Nourishing the wholeness of who we are

***

Sit a while

And welcome your Wise Woman

Welcome the parts you have ignored, neglected, that are unloved

Sit with them

Listen to their stories

For in their turmoil is a beautiful treasure to be discovered

***

Love them

Hold them

Forgive and let go

Let Love's embrace dissolve all transgressions

Bring home the lessons and gifts to your heart

Let them serve to nourish your inner garden

Composting, transforming, awakening the New

***

Light is born from darkness

New seeds grow from your well-tended garden

Nurtured by your love

Welcome all that is to become

Allow the rest to fall away

Naturally, easily, effortlessly

***

I am whole

I am Love

I am Peace

I AM

Waiting to rise in the Light of a frosty new dawn.

CHAPTER 10

Winter is a Yin Time

For many, the darkness of winter is a difficult time, creating low mood and apathy. For me, I love to look at this phase as a gift from Mother Nature, an opportunity to slow down, rest and heal, ready to regenerate for the following Spring.

As the trees gracefully let go of their leaves and become bare, Nature withdraws inside to sleep and dream of the coming Spring. It is an ideal opportunity for us to let go of unnecessary heavy baggage too and heal those parts of ourselves that have become neglected, or that are hidden.

Winter is a Yin time, a feminine space to receive, to withdraw, to slow down, to nourish and nurture our inner world. It is here that we connect with our inner Crone and Wise Woman.

Winter is the beginning of our journey, for all is born out of the void of darkness. We know that the Spiral of Life is always contracting, expanding, and contracting. Winter is a time of contraction. A space that allows us to let go and to nestle into our inner cave and feel cocooned. We can see this mirrored in our own menstrual cycle as our 'Inner Winter.'

Winter is our foundation from which all is birthed and eventually blossoms. When we fully surrender to this phase, we touch the deeper realms and mysteries of our dark feminine power.

During Winter, it may seem like nothing is happening. It can feel a place of emptiness, but this could not be further from the truth. Deep gestational impulses are occurring on a subtle level, as we connect with the void of infinite possibilities.

With practice, sinking and listening deeper within allows us to feel the wisdom of the inner stillness we are experiencing.

Winter allows us to feel nourished, supported and held.

Can you allow yourself to now slow down and breathe? Listen inwards to what your body is telling you?

What message does she have for you today?

It takes a strong mind and courageous heart to say, 'NO,' to honour our inner need for rest and quietness.

Instead of dreading the short days and lack of light, and pushing through to get things done, I invite you to slow down and nourish your inner landscape.

We are both dark and light, and darkness is a natural part of the overall cycle of death and rebirth.

Imagine the dark velvety softness enveloping you, holding and nurturing you right now.

Just like day follows night, like Spring follows Winter, we re-remember what it means to live in flow with the rhythms and seasons. This is our natural state of being that offers such richness and depth for our soul. The body yearns to slow down too. Do you feel that?

In the story of Winter, we gather our resources deep within, embrace our shadow, peel back the layers to see what we are ready to let go of, inviting the *treasures* of our shadow to shape our rebirth, our future hopes, and dreams.

We transform the weeds of our unconscious habits, allowing ourselves to grieve, to rest in stillness and dream of the woman we are becoming. A flower doesn't bloom all year. It has its perfect moment of glory, when all the conditions are right for it to shine and radiate its magnificence. I invite you to lean into Mother Earth's Winter wisdom and her natural gift of death and renewal.

When we embrace our dark feminine, we accept the wholeness of who we are.

The Descent into Winter

After the exuberance of Summer activity and heat, there is a deep quietening of the Earth as she withdraws her life force inwards ready for the darker months of the year. We are led deep into Autumn. Fallen leaves create a beautiful mosaic of reds, orange and yellow colour on the ground, creating a damp carpet for composting and nourishment, ready for the next cycle. The seeds of our harvest live on during the dormancy of Winter, ready to grow and renew once again in the Spring.

Mother Earth is calling us too. Do you feel her? She invites us to begin our journey inwards, to begin our descent into Winter and prepare ourselves to embrace our dark feminine nature. First, we must cross the threshold of Samhain.

Samhain – The Festival of Death and Remembrance

Samhain is the Celtic Festival celebrated on 31st October. It is here we are invited to cross the threshold, a transition from the old to the new, what the Celts mark as the end of the energetic year and the beginning of the next year and our descent into the dark months of Winter.

For the Celts, the day did not begin at dawn, it began at sunset, with darkness.

It is the final harvest consisting of nuts and berries, representing the end of the cycle of growth as we now enter the death cycle. The seeds of the harvest fall into the dark Earth and lie there, seemingly dormant, until the return of the Light at the Winter Solstice. Seeds then begin to slowly push themselves upwards towards the growing light, ready to sprout in the coming Spring.

The Sun God goes underground with the seed, until the return of the Light. Meanwhile, the Goddess has reign of the land. In her form as the Crone, she dominates the dark phase and brings her wisdom and healing to bear. Darkness is fertile with potential for the coming Spring.

This transition, between what was, and what is to become, creates a thinning of the veils between the world of matter and spirit. This is when we connect most closely with our ancestors and loved ones who have passed over to the other side. They are close now and it is a good time to honour their passing, to celebrate their gifts and wisdom that still lives on within our own blood and bones. It is a time to heal the ancestral 'wounds,' and traumas that have gone unacknowledged, unseen, unforgiven, that now call for healing, forgiveness, witness, and transformation.

Journey with me in chapter 11, as I share my Samhain Ritual for this turning of the Wheel.

CHAPTER 11.
Samhain
Honouring our Ancestors

My Personal Samhain Ritual – 'On the Precipice of Change'

Sitting on the brink of change, I feel the magic and anticipation of a new cycle.

I prepare myself to sit quietly in meditation, to receive the magic of this opening. I gather my things in honour of my ancestors and light a candle. I call upon the Four Directions and the Great Grandmother, of All Time, the Mother of All. I take a couple of deep breaths signalling to my body that I am going into meditation, simultaneously letting go of all distractions.

I am surrounded by the comforting darkness of my healing space, except for the occasional flicker of soft, warm candlelight. Soon my breathing deepens, and I find myself deep within my womb cave, now a familiar space of comfort. I'm immediately aware of the shift in my consciousness. A welcoming hand reaches forward through time to take hold of mine. An ancient hand that holds the secrets and wisdom of the old Earth, as She once was. I feel the comfort of an all-pervading presence holding me. My heart softens and opens to receive the immense love flowing to me.

I feel the presence of my ancestors close to me. Our ancestors knew the trials of earthly life – what it took to stay strong in the face of adversity. I feel the wisdom of our primal ancestors, who knew how to dedicate a life to living in rightful relationship with the world around them, through heartfelt gratitude for all Life. They recognised that they were part of Life itself and that if they neglected, took advantage, or caused harm to another or the Earth herself, then they too would fall out of balance, and ill fortune would plague their lives. They would listen to the pulse of the Earth's heartbeat and seek wisdom from the heavenly stars for potent signs of change and would prepare and align themselves with these, to flow in harmony.

Once again, I find myself sitting around a huge fire in circle with my ancestors. Loved ones who have passed over, reach forward piercing the veil. I feel the sweetness of their love touch my heart and nourish my inner being. Tears gently flow as I receive waves of love, too much for my precious heart to hold.

I am surrounded by my elders, spiritual ancestors, those who are here to teach me, remind me of who I truly am. They come to support me in letting go of those struggles and pains that would keep me small and separate from the glory of unconditional love.They encourage me to live my dreams. I heard them say, "Let go of your doubt, your judgement and fear; loosen the tethers of their grip."

I feel their loving presence build around me, strengthening me, inviting me to open my heart even wider. I am encouraged to voice out loud what is ready to be released, not only within my own life but in the lives of my ancestral lineage – those energetic threads and bonds that run deep in my blood and bones.

The fire in my heart grows stronger and brighter. The heat almost unbearable, as it begins to burn through resistance and the critical voices of doubt and unworthiness. I feel pain in the back of my heart – aargh, I let out a groan as the past is transmuted in love's flame. Tears flow unhindered now, as I let go.Tears of sadness trickle down my cheeks, as I surrender to all that is ready to fall away. I declare, 'The time is now to let go, to forgive.'

Gradually I feel the pain dissolve and my heart and chest begin to relax and soften. I send my expanded heart flame down each paternal line, first my mother line and then my father line. I command my fierce love down to the root of all separation and back to the beginning of time, of creation. The time when we were all One as Divine sparks of pure light, untainted by fear, by control, by greed, by hatred. I breathe this light seed up and back into my heart, knowing this primal Light of creation has touched all the hearts in our lineage. I breathe out, a liberating breath, sending onwards a wave of love to our future generations. And so, a new seed is planted for the future. I feel the warmth of pink love, like candyfloss, move through me and down and up the line. I feel peace.

I stay like this for some time allowing myself to soften and everything to sink in. I know I am changed at a deep level. Another layer has been released, feeling the sweet liberation as a bird flies free from its cage.

I give thanks to my ancestors and elders. I feel such joy and gratitude fill my heart – the feeling is mutual within our circle. The celebration begins. I see smiling faces, lit up by the central fire, that now dance and sway, rejoicing in love's truth and liberation. The sound of a familiar drumbeat resonates in my bones, and I feel its rhythm move me, reminding me of how it feels to be of Earth and to be united with soul family.

Gradually after some time, I hear the muted sounds of saucepans clink in our kitchen, as I imagine our teenage son begins to cook. The visions and the internal sounds dissipate, and I become more aware of my own body sitting in my room.

I gently return and become still. I feel soft and light, as if a weight has been lifted from me. My hands move slowly over my body – touching and caressing my legs, my arms, then I stroke my belly, appreciating it's inner beauty and power.

Finally, my hands come to rest on my heart in gratitude. I am now fully present in my own sacred space where two large candles with soft, warm flames, gently flicker in recognition.

You may like to create your own Samhain Ritual to honour your Ancestors. You'll find at the end of this chapter the 'Blood and Bone Samhain Ritual' as guidance for you to follow.

Symbols for Samhain

Cauldron

The cauldron is closely associated with Samhain. It is the cosmic container for all life and death, transformation, and rebirth. It is considered the Holy Grail that carries the potential of the Divine Feminine and the sacredness of life.

The Besom Broom

The broom is used both practically and symbolically to sweep away the old energy, to create a clear space for new beginnings. Just like we sweep away old dying leaves, we can use the Broom to sweep away limiting conditions, past worries and stresses, old behaviour patterns and heavy energy. This allows our life force to rise and regenerate.

Acorns

From small acorns magnificent Oak trees grow. Acorns represent wisdom, longevity, and good fortune. All nuts carry the pure potential and gifts of the mother tree.

Rosemary

Twigs of Rosemary are used for remembrance and cleansing the spirit. You can have these as part of your sacred space. Remember to honour the Rosemary plant by asking for permission before taking or cutting sprigs.

Colours

Samhain colours tend to include:

Black, to represent the dark phase and death.
Orange, for vitality.
Purple, for wisdom and insight.

You may feel inspired to gather some of these items together in expression of this phase you are moving through. As you walk with Mother Nature, notice how She feels in your body. Welcome her here within your blood and bones. Open your senses to receive her wisdom through the sounds of the trees in the wind, noticing the plants and trees that are dying back. Notice how they may mirror aspects of yourself that you are ready to shed.

Samhain Rituals - Honouring our Ancestors

Family Candle Ceremony

A simple ceremony you might like to do with your family is to honour the passing of loved ones, including pets.

Gather in a circle and give a small candle, tealight to each of you who is attending.

In the centre, have ready a fireproof plate/container that will safely hold the candles once lit.

I would suggest one person takes the lead to invite your ancestors into the space.

"We welcome our departed loved ones who have crossed the rainbow bridge, into our home. We honour your presence here with us."

Take it in turn to say how you remember your loved one. Light a single candle in honour of them.

For example,

"I remember Uncle Sam for his humour and generous heart...."

You will finish with a plateful of beautiful lit candles and the fond memories of loved ones that warms the heart and fills the room.

To close your circle, you might like to say,

"I give thanks to our Ancestors' presence, wisdom and love, and we send you our blessings for your onward journey, as we now close this circle. Blessed Be."

Samhain Rituals – Honouring our Ancestors

Blood and Bone Samhain Ritual

Celebrating Samhain helps remind us to give gratitude to what we have received in our harvest, not just in the fields but also with our own personal harvests of achievements, personal growth, lessons, and milestones.

Create your sacred space with items that hold significance for you.

Gather together –

- Dark or black cloth representing the dark cycle
- Two candles to represent your mother and father lineage
- Additional candle for your future generations if you feel so inclined
- Items that represent your mother and father lineage such as, old photos, jewellery, crystals/stones, their favourite flowers
- Ancestor Dolls – you may choose to make your own ancestor doll which is a powerful way to honour your mother and father. These can be simply made with natural materials that call you on your Nature walks, or more elaborate made of cloth (see chapter on *Honouring our Ancestors* for more suggestions)
- Incense or white sage for burning
- Cauldron or fireproof container to burn old papers or things written that you wish to let go of in your life.
- Have a journal and pen to hand, to note down any insights and guidance you receive.
- Before you begin, note your intentions, any questions you might have, requests for healing. On a separate piece of paper (that you can burn later), write down what you wish to release and let go of.

Once your sacred space is set up, prepare yourself to go into meditation by inviting long, deep breaths to settle your mind and centre yourself in your body.

Call upon the Five Directions of Earth, Air, Fire, Water and Great Spirit (see earlier chapter 9 on *Creating Sacred Space*).

Call upon the Great Grandmother of All Time, the Mother of All, and the all-knowing presence of the Dark Feminine. I often call upon Cerridwen, a Welsh Goddess, Keeper of the Sacred Cauldron, to work with during Autumn/Winter. I share more about Cerridwen later in the chapter 12 *Our Inner Cave and Sanctuary*.

Call upon your ancestors to come close to meet you in sacred space around the ethereal fire.

Enjoy a communion with your ancestors and spirit guides. See who wants to step forward for you to connect with.

You may see or you may just have a strong sense of their comforting presence, love, and strength.

Many of our shadow aspects of fear, sadness, grief, anger, and pain, have come down our lineage, due to their trauma and limiting beliefs that we still carry in our blood and bones.

We are in a position now to heal our ancestry. We have the time, resources, and awareness to do this when our ancestors didn't have.

Fear of judgement was a core family wound. Over many years I have worked to clear this pattern that has run in my life, benefitting both my ancestral lineage, myself and our son and daughter in the process.

Reflect upon your own life and the story of your ancestors –

- What needs to be honoured, their gifts and strengths as well as their difficulties?
- What situations, traumas need honouring and forgiving?

Become aware of any limiting tendencies you are carrying. Feel the emotion behind these and how they play out in your life. Acknowledge and honour these with compassion, asking for forgiveness.

We can continue to hold much emotional pain from childhood, so allow space in your heart to feel, forgive and begin to let them go.

Voicing out loud what you wish to heal and let go of, is very powerful. Coming from an open heart declare...

"I now choose to honour, forgive, and release these patterns of fear (name whatever is coming up) ......and allow the healing balm of unconditional love to flow through my blood and bones, down my mother and father line and to all future generations."

Repeat as necessary, being guided by your own intuition and the presence of your ancestors.

Embracing these emotions in this way, helps to loosen their grip on us bringing more freedom to our authentic expression.

Ancestors encourage us to let go and to receive their wisdom and love. They want us to live our full potential and to fulfil our dreams, especially so if the dreams of our ancestors weren't fulfilled.

Sit for as long as needed to feel complete.

Give your thanks, then gradually bring your awareness back to your own environment.

If you haven't already, place any written note or papers that you wish to burn in the cauldron. You may choose to burn this at a different time, when you can be outside to safely burn the contents.

Bury the ashes ceremonially by intending that Mother Earth receives them to compost and transform in her body of light and giving thanks to the Earth for offering her gift of transformation.

Samhain Journal Quesiions

Reflect upon the past year up to this point –

1. What significant achievements and changes did you make personally?

2. What are you proud of about yourself? Breathe these feelings into your heart.

3. What things challenged you?

4. What have been the lessons and gifts of these challenges?

5. What emotions and belief patterns are you ready to heal and let go of?

6. Who needs to be forgiven – include yourself?

7. How will you ensure to slow down and rest more?

CHAPTER 12:
Our Inner Cave and Sanctuary

Our womb space is our place of power, a potent space of creativity, of death and rebirth. She is our Inner Cave and Cauldron, a sanctuary to come and rest during Winter. She calls us deep within to heal, to let go, to rest and dream of what new is emerging.

Just as we turn over Summer's dying blooms and prune back our gardens, to lay our soil to rest, and plant seeds ready for next spring, our inner Cave carries the same potential.

Winter is the foundation from which all is birthed and
eventually blossoms.

When the old dies, the womb is prepared for the new, just like we experience as part of our menstrual cycle, our 'Inner Winter'.

Our 'Inner Winter' Womb Cycle

During our 'Inner Winter' bleed we contract to fulfil our inner needs and desires. We are naturally more sensitive because we are more open and permeable to Universal energies, psychic and intuitive impressions and the flow of creative ideas. Even if we no longer menstruate, women still experience the power and sensations of this cycle.

Our Inner Winter is known as one of the most creative and powerful phases for women. It is the gateway to deeply connecting with our Wise Woman archetype.

A helpful affirmation to hold in our heart and womb when we bleed is:

"When I bleed, I am in full flow with my feminine power and my connection to the wisdom of the Earth brings me home to self."

In ancient times, women on their bleed would often isolate themselves from society so they could 'tune in' to their creative inner voice and power. They would do this together, communing to support and nurture each other, giving space for inner reflection. This is where the name 'red tent' has come from. Women would give their blood as an offering and gift to Mother Earth to deepen the bond between them and the powerful Mother Creator of all life. This became a sacred ritual of communion with the Earth. There is an Oracle stone in the Abbey Grounds in Glastonbury, Somerset, UK, an oval stone that women long ago, would sit upon to bleed and gift their red blood to Mother Earth. It was recognised as a time of sacred communion with the Earth Mother and the Cosmic Heavens. Women were known to receive inspiration from the Cosmos as when we bleed our psychic and intuitive abilities are more pronounced.

Some women still do this today, by offering their blood as a gift to the Earth to honour their Earth Mother and their relationship with her. Today Red Tent circles are held for women to come together to share and empower each other, holding the same intent although not necessarily bleeding together.

We can use this time of Winter to go within, to honour our true feelings and let go of those things that are ready to die and fall away, to be composted to become fertiliser for our new creations. This is a powerful phase of transformation and alchemy as we literally shed physically and emotionally, the last cycle.

This process allows our womb to become bare and ripe, ready for impregnating with new seeds, ideas, and dream projects.

We can create a field of abundant fertility through our loving presence and self-nourishment practices.

The Cauldron of Transformation

The Cauldron of Transformation is a metaphor for working with our womb energy during the dark phase.

At Samhain, I bring out my black cauldron and begin working with Her consciously and my Inner Cave. She sits in my sacred space as a constant reminder and invitation to go within, to connect with my Inner Cave, to release and transform the old energies that are no longer needed. I work with the Cauldron in simple ritual and ceremony. I write down what I am ready to release and offer it to the Cauldron to burn and then bury the ashes with sacred intention, in our garden or the woods.

Goddess Archeiypes

There are different Goddess archetypes that we can call upon to help support us in this phase of death and renewal.

Personally, I love to work with the Celtic Goddess of the Underworld, Cerridwen, Keeper of the Cauldron of sacred knowledge, inspiration, of death and rebirth. According to Welsh legend, she was Mother to Taliesin, the greatest Welsh poet, and is recognised as a white witch and Goddess of poetry, inspiration, and the cauldron of transfiguration.

'She labours continually at Her cauldron, stirring up the forces of inspiration, Divine knowledge and the eternal cycle of birth, death, and rebirth. She is the Wheel of Life. She is also associated with the sow and grain. The sow symbolises good luck and spiritual growth. Grain symbolises abundance and nurturance.'

She sits in her cave, with her cauldron, inviting us to enter and let go all that is ready to go. She helps us face our shadow, encouraging us to confront unhelpful egoic patterns that are ready to die. She stirs her pot whilst singing and chanting, weaving magic as she does. She is a strong, loving wise woman elder and I feel completely 'held' and loved by her when I am moving through deep change.

Cerridwen's Spirit Animals

I associate the mystical black Crow with Cerridwen. Crow is the messenger of Spirit and will journey between our world of matter and the spirit world to convey messages and to guide us. Listen out for Crow's caw and his magical eye for signs of prophecy. Crow and Raven, also part of the same family, are the bringers of magic, helping us see the gifts and lessons of the darkness as Crow/Raven sees all.

Cerridwen is also associated with the Owl – a night eagle who swoops silently on the wing in the dark of the night. With the ability to see the minutest pray in the dark we can use its keen eyesight and heightened senses to see through illusion and to seek the wisdom and gifts of the dark phase.

Kali Ma is a Hindu Goddess of Death and Rebirth, a Dark Mother of creation, and destruction and consort to Lord Shiva. Kali sprang from the third eye of Durga, a fierce Warrior Goddess, who wanted to rid the world of demons. Many tales of Kali portray violent scenes of blood and death, and her dancing wildly over the deceased. She embodies the dark power and ferocity of the Great Goddess, and it is often our own power that we fear the most.

When we look at the underlying message of her energy, she is helping us face our greatest fears and inner demons so that we can transform them and fully realise our potential.

Explore what Goddesses you are drawn to. You may like to choose to work with one so you can become familiar with their healing energy and wisdom to support you in embracing the dark phase. *Awaken your Goddess* by Liz Simpson explores the myths and legends of fifteen Goddess archetypes from a selection of cultures to help women understand how they can be applied practically in their own lives.

You can read about one woman's shamanic journey that I guided to connect with Cerridwen and her Cauldron of Transformation. Her journey helped to transform old dense energy and to awaken new possibilities. You can find her journey next – 'The Golden Apple' by Kirsty Garland.

Listen to Sheffy Oren Bach's Grandmother Song on Spotify. Link can be found at the back of the book under Resources.

A Woman's Story

The Golden Apple by Kirsty Garland

Back in 2019, I guided Kirsty on a shamanic journey to connect with her Inner Cave and the Cauldron of Transformation. This is her journey as told by Kirsty.

I was taken to a tree that had, for want of other words, appeared to have been blown apart. It appeared to me as bleak, twisted in attempts to grow in the darkness that it existed in. A dingy dampness lingered...that smell of the old as it begins to rot and decompose.

As we drew closer, it became apparent that there were in fact two sides to this tree. One half had been blown open through the trauma that it had experienced, covered in layers of web like protection, home to the spider that protected what lay inside. Inside...who knows what...for it is too dark to really see, and who would want to anyway?

On closer inspection the other half was healthy – as if two sides of a coin, reflecting back to me that light and darkness exist simultaneously. The stories no longer relevant; it is a presentation in front of me of the reality of dualism – that where there is darkness there is also light. This was demonstrated by a thin veil of shimmering light. I can literally step in and out of each side, choose either reality, or ignore either reality. I could ignore...or I could embrace what is mine and bring it into wholeness.

The decision was to go into the tree – to climb in through the exposed opening. This did take some encouragement and there was initial resistance, an inner knowing perhaps that the familiar terrain might change, rather than fearing what was actually there.

As the decision was made, our journey began...nothing was as fearsome as it first seemed. We journeyed down through the layers and into the ground, down through two levels, right to the bottom, an earthy space, brown in its hues, dusty and basic in appearance. There is no need for frills here. I was guided to see the 'Mother' there, old and wise stirring her magic – directing me and showing me what needs to be done for the moment.

I moved up a level and clearly was shown these 'rotten apples' attached to the roots of the tree. Under direction, we worked to clear them, and found a shoot (like a garbage shoot) that takes them down into the ground, into the transformational energy that clears. Down they all went, and some of the roots with them, all the rotten energy cleared and swept away; some time was spent but it was good time.... it was safe time.

Down again to the lower level and I'm joined by an owl again, swooping and illuminating any more areas that need to be cleared. My bear is with me, protecting and keeping a watchful eye while I'm sweeping again – clearing and letting go.

A thin rod of light pokes up through the ground. As it gains momentum, it pushes up through to the other levels, creating now a shaft of light. And suddenly I'm aware that there is lots of light coming in – not just gold but, purples and pinks and gentle blues – all the rainbow, descending from the heavens and being pulled down through the trunk and into even these lower levels.

My 'old mother' is there collecting the debris and stirring her cauldron. She chants and as she stirs, she has intent and magic. She is thankful for the old as she has the magic to transform, she has the magic to grow the new. With her song and her intent, she gives a new energy to the dark swampy mixture, and it begins to take a new form, a new hue...it begins to turn gold. As it spins and it weaves, it becomes brighter and clearer. She sings her magic and is jubilant. The owl too is jubilant, and the bear protects and supervises, as the process is complete, the transformation is done.

The mother looks at me and thanks me for honouring her work, allowing her to complete her destiny and fulfil the transformation of the old into the new. She pulls a gift out of the cauldron – a golden apple that shines – it glows. "For you for your hard work."

I eat it, feeling the colour digest and assimilate within my energy, glowing, the promise of what is to come. It's time to journey up again. The tree is clear, the way is clear. The tree is encased in golden energy, honouring both the darkness and the light in all of us. Out of the tree, a smaller tree is growing, a branch of new growth reaching up. New young fresh.

Well...time has elapsed since this but in the end, it turned out to be very symbolic in many ways. Firstly, I wanted to say that it has become painstakingly clear to me that healing is an ongoing process. In many ways this felt like a journey that has held my hand over those last few years and is still giving me hope and encouragement.

I was right to feel reluctance at the start...to be cautious about making the step because much of what has followed has been gut wrenchingly difficult. A detox of the essence of myself...and anyone who has done a good detox knows how difficult it can be!

I'd love to say I just let go of everything and then it was clear sailing...but as it turns out it was a series of layers...some painful...some excruciating...some beautiful. The gift has been in taking the time to honour the past. To unwrap tenderly... to allow and make space with a deep compassion for what could not be seen or felt before. There is a newfound sense of an embodied self; a readiness to look inwards rather than outwards for answers. I would say that as fear has been felt and processed out of the nervous system there is a greater sense of respect, kindness end empathy.

So often we are told that there is no light without shadow but in this case the opposite is more appropriate...Sometimes it is only as we find and recognise the shadow that we make space for the light, and the path to wholeness becomes clearer. *"An honouring of both the darkness and light in all of us"*

Kirsty Garland

Mediiaiion io Your Inner Cave

Create a quiet sacred space where you won't be disturbed.

Settle yourself down and make yourself comfortable either sitting or lying with your knees bent and your feet flat.

Invite some nice long deep breaths and sigh out, allowing any sounds of tiredness, yawning, releasing to happen naturally.

Connect with your heart by placing one hand on your chest in loving presence. Breathe a couple of breaths here, opening, softening and relaxing.

Feel your back supported, relaxing your shoulders and hips down towards the ground. Feel yourself connect to Mother Earth beneath you, grounding your roots deep down.

Place a hand on your belly to guide your breathing and connect more deeply here.

Begin to slow your breathing, taking soft, gentle, and deep breaths into your belly like you used to as a baby.

When you are ready, imagine dropping into the cave of your womb space. Imagine you are going deep inside to sit in the centre of your cave.

With your senses awake, feel, and look around your inner cave space.

What does it feel like? What do you notice? Observe rather than judge or make meaning. Let go of any expectation of what she will be like to you.

Allow yourself to rest in here for a while.

If emotions and feelings surface, welcome them. If you feel a sense of love, pleasure and connection, welcome them. Receive any images with open curiosity and a sense of play. All is welcome.

Acknowledge all that you discover with love, compassion, and appreciation.

You may wish to gift your Inner Cave something that shares your love, appreciation, compassion. What gift of love would you like to offer her?

When you are ready to bring your meditation to a close, give your thanks for her presence and affirming that you will be back to explore some more.

Take some long deep breaths and begin to feel your body sitting or lying. Become aware of the sensations of your body, the clothes you are wearing, your temperature and your surroundings.

Gradually bring yourself back into the present moment, opening your eyes slowly to adjust to the light.

The first time you do this, it may be just enough to connect and sense what is here. You don't have to do anything. Being present and connected is just enough.

Another time, you may want to explore a little deeper. We explore deeper in the Wise Woman Meditation, in the next chapter.

Journal Prompts

1. If you have done the Guided Meditation to your Inner Cave, capture any feelings and impressions straight away.

2. What does your Inner Cave look and feel like; describe what you see.

3. Take some colouring pens or paints and see what colours and shapes want to flow on to paper as an expression of her beauty and wisdom or what may need healing.

4. Reflect in your journal what this feels like to connect with your womb and Inner Cave. Feel any emotions that may arise and embrace them, inviting you to wrap your arms around yourself in a loving hug.

5. What healing needs to occur and what difference would this make to your life? You can use the descriptions you have imagined in words or pictures as a symbolic way to connect with what needs healing.

For example, I was supporting a woman to reconnect with her womb. Initially, it was murky and dark but gradually as we brought healing energy into the area and she worked with intention, her womb began to become brighter and lighter, flowers started to grow and blossom, and a warm fire began to burn in the centre.

CHAPTER 13:
Our Wise Woman/Crone

Winter is a time to honour the Crone or what we also call the Wise Woman. The Crone is also known as the old Hag, often depicted with silver hair, wearing a dark cloak, embodying wisdom from all her life experiences, stirring her cauldron of transformation. Her powerful presence can be felt, having gained her strength through learning the lessons of life's challenges. She now offers her wisdom to her community, supporting younger women to become empowered and strong.

I am now in my Crone years, and I feel this is my time to pass on my wisdom through these words.

How Do We Connect with Our Wise Woman?

When we relax and sink down into our womb space and connect with our Inner Cave, we can begin to tap into the deep stillness that resides within. It is within, that we will begin to hear our inner voice, the voice and impulses of our inner knowing and intuition – the Wise Woman at the centre of our Cave. She already knows the answers we seek and the questions we need to ask ourselves. She knows when it is time to rest and be patient, knowing the right time to emerge will come.

> *Do not be afraid of the silence, for it is this deepening within*
> *that guides us to intuit the strong impulses of our inner*
> *knowing.*

Our Wise Woman knows when something feels off balance with a situation or another person.

Can you recall a situation when you have felt something intuitively is not right, but couldn't explain the reasons?

You may not be able to articulate a logical reason, but your instinct may be telling you to avoid, delay or wait before deciding or acting. On the other hand, your instincts could be telling you to act now, take the plunge, yet your logical mind is questioning. With practice, we can focus inside to the subtle signals of our body and learn to trust our inner knowing.

What past or current situation comes to mind, where you could apply this approach?

Our Wise Woman holds her inner council and is not afraid to follow her own truth and path even if it may appear she is walking alone. She is never truly alone as she is walking with knowing and with the connection to the heart of the great Earth Mother, her fingers on the pulse of Life. She learns to listen to the potent signs from her friends in Nature – the birds, animals, trees, and elemental spirits. She treads a path between both worlds, of spirit and our everyday world, bringing through the wisdom and magic to support her in her mission to nurture her community. This is likely to be sharing her life's wisdom, educating, teaching, and nourishing those who are ready and thirsty to learn and grow more.

Because of our patriarchal history, we do not readily connect with our inner Wise Woman. Our inner voice can feel muffled and unclear because there has been too much confusion around our value and worth. But she is eager to connect with us now, our She power is awakening.

Mother Earth is calling us to take the journey to remember the truth and wisdom of who we truly are.

Wise Woman Mediiaiion

Take some time now to find a quiet space, to connect with Her.

Create a safe space where you won't be interrupted.

Have your journal and pen to hand, in case you receive any insights.

Sit on the floor or in a chair, planting your feet on the ground. Alternatively, if you prefer, you can lie down with your knees bent.

When you are relaxed and comfortable, start by taking some long deep breaths down into your body and belly.

Open your heart to receive your womb (see the Heart/Womb Meditation in Part One and on my website for guidance).

As you come into the centre of your womb space, know this is your Inner Cave, your inner sanctuary.

Imagine you are lighting a candle in the centre of the space. Breathe deeply into your belly, inviting the warmth to spread into your hips.

When you feel ready, call upon your Wise Woman.

Depending on what's going on for you at the time, she may appear readily before you or she may be in the shadows. You may see colours, shapes, or an outline of a form, depending how she wants to show herself to you. If you are not particularly visual you may not see her, but you may sense a growing presence in your womb space. Just rest and listen with all your senses, with a loving presence. Be open and without expectation.

You may find there is silence, and this is how she wishes to connect with you, in stillness.

You may experience sensations or tension. Breathe a little deeper into these places, inviting yourself to soften and relax. Welcome all.

You may wish to drop a question into your Cave. What would you like to ask her?

Such as:

What can you share and teach me about myself?

What do I need to know in this moment?

How do I know when my wise woman is present?

What needs healing or releasing in my life?

Alternatively, she may have a lot to say, having been waiting for you to connect with her. She may share emotions of sadness, anger, for having been disowned by society for so long. You may find you feel emotional as you reconnect with her, as you reclaim this fundamental part of you.

Before you are ready to return, give thanks to your wise woman.

Take a few deep breaths, gradually becoming aware of your fingers and toes, gradually inviting your body to wake up.

Become aware of your surroundings and give your belly and hips and heart a wonderful loving stroke with your hands before fully awakening.

You can find a Guided Meditation on my website, link can be found at the back of the book under Resources.

I know when I first connected deeply with my womb, it felt like a deep home coming to myself. Tears of joy, relief and grief came, and I allowed them to flow. When these quietened, I felt an immense peace, contentment and joy move through me. My healing of my womb had just begun but the trust was now there.

We are each unique, so learn to be patient and kind with yourself. There is no right or wrong way to do this.

Practice each day for a few days, then take a break.

Listen to this beautiful song written and sung by Elaine Cullinane who attended a few of my women's circles.

Wise Woman Song – 'Woman Deep Down in the Woods' by Elaine Cullinane. Link can be found at the back of the book under Resources.

Journal Prompts

It is helpful to do the meditation above first so that you are connected to her energy. Settle into the stillness of your womb so that answers can rise intuitively from this place.

1. If there is a particular issue or challenge in your life, what would your Wise Woman's response be to this? Can she offer a different perspective?

2. What are you being called to do for yourself?

3. What steps do you need to take to trust in the voice of your Wise Woman and let go of the external 'noise'?

4. How do you need to self-nourish?

CHAPTER 14

Treasures in Our Shadow

'One does not become enlightened by imagining figures of light, but by making the darkness conscious.' Carl Jung

Winter is an ideal opportunity for us to let go of unnecessary heavy baggage and heal those parts of ourselves that have become neglected, or that we may have hidden. This is what we call our shadow. Our shadow that follows us around, yet when we look behind it is nowhere to be seen.

The shadow is part of our unconscious, consisting of those parts of ourselves that we are blind to, or are out of our current field of vision. They don't usually come into full view until we are confronted with a situation that triggers old emotions and memories. We then find we are acting and behaving from a 'wounded' place within us, often because of early traumatic childhood experiences that are too painful to deal with at the time.

Growing up, many of us didn't feel safe to express our emotions and certainly wouldn't have had the skill set to handle and effectively process them. I know that was certainly the case for me. I did not feel safe to express my emotions and would end up running into my bedroom to hide and cry. For most of us, these experiences get buried deep within us.

Amazingly, we create coping mechanisms and behaviours to help us adapt and survive that have served us well. But as we grow older and wiser, we recognise something is missing. There comes a point when what kept us safe becomes a hindrance to moving forwards in our life and in our relationships. What used to be helpful no longer applies and we have the choice to take the journey inwards to embrace our shadow – our fears, hurts, anger and sadness – and bring them home to our heart for healing and forgiveness. In this way we embrace our wholeness.

Why Would We Want to Befriend Our Shadow?

Although for the most part our shadow is hidden, it still has a powerful impact on our daily quality of life.

Do you feel a part of you is missing?

Do you feel a heavy weight that you are burdened with, causing you to feel drained?

Perhaps those limiting beliefs keep tripping you up and are still influencing how you show up in your relationships and with your work?

Or perhaps you feel a niggle, that you can't put your finger on, but it unsettles you and you don't feel complete?

Many people keep themselves busy as a way of avoiding facing these hidden parts.

Is this something you can relate to?

Sometimes there are parts of ourselves that we would rather ignore and keep quiet.

In truth our shadow is our friend. By keeping the shadow hidden, it takes more of our energy to keep painful emotions suppressed, causing us to feel heavy and tired. Longstanding avoidance can ultimately create imbalance in our health and vitality.

When we embrace our shadow and love and accept all, we recognise our wholeness and begin to feel more comfortable in our own skin. We become our true authentic Self that is fundamentally Love.

Let's Get Personal with Our Shadow

Our soul's wisdom knows exactly what we need for our personal and spiritual growth. External events with other people often trigger old memories that are brought to the surface. This may be an interaction with someone that has stirred up lots of emotion or something that has caused you to go into a downward spiral. Experiences that trigger painful emotions that are greater than perhaps the situation warrants, is a signal to work with our shadow. It's a calling from within to heal an old wound and pattern that is still running in our life.

When I broke my foot over Easter 2021, initially I had to rely on my husband for support. He already did his fair share around the house, and through his body language I could feel this added pressure was taking its toll on him, causing him stress. This added to the vulnerable feeling inside of me that already felt a bit guilty for being an added burden. There came a point when these emotions became too much for me and tears overflowed. I realised this deep hurt I was experiencing was coming from my 'wounded self' that had been triggered as I would have often felt a burden to my mum who was always busy.

As young children we are like sponges, taking in everything that is going on in our environment. We haven't yet developed the filters to discern what is ours and what belongs to others. This can set up belief patterns of blame and taking on responsibility for others' experiences, something we can choose to unlearn in later life.

Over the years when I have found myself in emotional pain, I would spend time with myself in meditation, knowing this was the best way to resolve, heal and forgive. I connect with my Higher Self and send love and compassion to my Inner Child until I feel a peace and acceptance descend within and around me. My Higher Self knows that other people's reactions and frustrations are not my responsibility but as a highly sensitive child and soul it was something that I found difficult. When we feel particularly vulnerable, early emotions rooted in childhood, can be triggered as we enter another level of the healing spiral. Many a time we find ourselves revisiting these painful memories. We may think we have completed our healing until the wounding is triggered again. This time we are invited to view things from a different perspective so we can heal, forgive and move on lighter and brighter.

You can do much energetically to shift a relationship just by working on your own trigger points and healing these so that you can return to a place of self-love. This automatically shifts the vibrations and frequency you are sending out to another, and they will feel that shift energetically too. Soul relationships increasingly come together in partnerships and families, to help each other heal and balance karma, therefore helping each other's soul to evolve and expand in consciousness.

A lot of the healing work I do with one-to-one clients focusses on healing relationships and fundamentally our relationship with our self. I've worked with a few clients who have had estranged relationships with their mother and father or siblings, some who had not been in touch with for many years.

Inner healing results in an energetic shift within the client's heart which sends out a new pulse and vibration. Instead of feeling bitter or resentful, needy, or fearful, they feel more love and compassion sometimes resulting in a surprising reconnection and renewal of harmony between family members.

Healing Patterns of Judgement

In Spring 2018, I was invited to run a Shamanic event using a local venue – I knew the owner very well both professionally and personally. The event was full and the energies that came through were very powerful. The following morning, the owner was in touch saying I had brought in some negative energies that he felt he needed to clear. Being a person of high integrity, I was distraught, feeling very worried about what might have happened and that I may have been the cause of this. This had never happened before. It didn't occur to me that he may be mistaken. I naturally assumed I was in the wrong.

At the time, I immediately apologised, sympathising with him and in doing so I was implying I was responsible. He was quite happy for this to be the case.

I recognised something big was being triggered – old feelings and patterns of guilt, of taking responsibility for having done something wrong when in fact I hadn't. I had reacted without first checking whether this was truth or in fact my truth. This was certainly a behaviour I experienced in my childhood and in my past lives.

After I had calmed down, I sought professional support with my Shamanic therapist I was seeing at the time. I was guided into a Shamanic Journey where I found myself sitting around a huge fire where there were several large Native American Chiefs. They held a very strong masculine presence which was both loving and wise. They invited me to explore the truth of what really happened. As I tuned in, I received strong images and a deep knowing of the truth which was confirmed by my therapist.

I had naturally given my power away to someone I perceived in authority because I was running a pattern of victim and accusation. In truth, he had been triggered by the powerful masculine energies that I had channelled that evening and didn't want to look at his own shadow of unhealed trauma.

When we are in denial, it is natural for us to look elsewhere to blame or project what we are experiencing and to look for other reasons for the cause of how we feel. Because my own pattern of self-judgement and blame was running as victim, I took it personally.

During this Shamanic Journey I had a big 'aha' moment and realisation of how this pattern had been running in my life. This was the gift, to realise my part in this dynamic and to reclaim my power and break the energetic chain.

Instantly I recognised this, the healing energies came pouring in, to soothe and alchemise the fear and transform the energy into love and forgiveness.

One does need to step back from the situation and see things from a higher perspective.

How often do we do that first?

The gift from my Higher Self was to see this pattern of persecution from a higher viewpoint so that I could heal at a deeper level. I moved from a place of self-judgement and being the victim of persecution to one of love, forgiveness, and compassion, most importantly with myself first.

Interestingly too, coming from this place there was no need to defend myself because I was not guilty and in that way the energy was diffused and something else became possible.

No further conversation about it was needed and the relationship between us continued to be amicable and harmonious.

The ripple effect across my life was fundamental in shifting my relationship with myself. In the few days that followed, I had people who had participated in the event but were unaware of this issue, come up to me to express their gratitude and to say how much they valued my help and benefitted from my healing that evening. They shared examples of how issues in their relationships had shifted significantly. This was another positive confirmation of the healing transformation I was experiencing.

There are many lifetimes where many of us have experienced persecution, the effects of this we still feel in our current life.

Have you noticed how what people say can trigger you into feelings of old hurt, anger and fear?

I invite you to reflect on your relationships and note what ones you feel triggered by or that cause you to feel irritated.

We can lose our sense of self and what is truth when this happens.

Personal Journal - Facing Our Shadows

"What is this darkness I have to face?" Bare, cold, desolate.

"Why, oh why, do I have to wade through darkness, for what purpose?" I ask.

Dampness clings to my ankles, pulling me down.

I will resist, I will pretend this is not happening.

Oh, this heaviness, "What is this?"

I take a deep breath and sigh out.

A gentle pause, almost surrendering, as if it's all too much effort.

"But what if I let go? Will I not sink and be devoured by the darkness?"

Oh, the fear is real – argh!

"What lurks in those shadows I do not want to see? I will turn a blind eye and look the other way. See, that is better."

"And yet, is it?"

This niggle, this presence in the shadows, creeping over my skin. I catch my breath in sheer terror of what I may find.

Then.... in the quiet corners of my mind I hear a soft gentle voice. A soothing voice that momentarily catches me in a moment of calm, putting an invisible wall between what was there and this moment.

And then I hear, "I am here with you. You are not alone. Do not move away."

I did not know where this voice came from or who spoke these words.

But I felt to linger some more in the shelter of these dulcet tones.

"I am holding you. Nothing is too great for me to bear. Lean into my arms and I will hold you safe in my Love. Together we can look into the shadows for it is not what you imagine it to be."

If it was for just hearing the words, I would have ignored and stayed firm in my resolve to resist going any further ...but it was the feeling of warmth that came over me and the subsequent softening of my body, of my limbs, my chest, that allowed me to stay in this space a little longer.

Tentatively, I began to relax a little, more confident in myself to look, feeling safe, knowing I could always run away again.

As if hearing my innermost thoughts, the voice said, "Why run away from yourself, child?" "What might happen if you stepped closer?"

Taking a deep breath I felt the soft presence of the voice beside me, giving me strength. I plucked up the courage and turned to face the shadows.

I found myself carrying a light, a light that seemed to come from the soft, gentle voice. This female presence was with me, standing by me. I was not alone.

Together, I became still and gradually more curious to look.

Expecting something gruesome and ugly to appear, peering through squinted eyes, I saw the outline of a shape emerge slowly from the shadows. Barely visible, I made out a figure, hunched and dark, except for a glimmer that was cast from the light in my hand.

The soft gentle voice whispered, "Reach out an invitation to that which stands before you."

In that moment, an idea slid into my mind to light a fire, that I and that 'thing' over there could sit by. Feeling the fire would give warmth and comfort and a focal point. It seemed as soon as I thought it, it had become. We were sitting close to the fire. It was comforting.

Gazing in the dim light, I asked the hunched, dark figure, "Who are you?"

In answer to my question, the figure stirred, the head lifting slightly up to reveal a youngish woman. Her face looked drawn, dark rings of sadness bore around her eyes, pain written in lines around her mouth. I was looking into a pair of frightened eyes, eyes that told the story of longing and abandonment.

Now it was my turn, that wanted to comfort and reassure. I began to realise this woman before me was a part of me.

Questions raced through my mind. "Had I disowned her, found her too difficult to bare?" "Were her emotions too hard to embrace, too heavy, too much?" Society would have me believe that. In the past, she would have been locked up, not fit for society, not belonging in the real world! But how could I turn my back on Her? I would not do that to a friend, so how could I do that to her, myself?

And yet I had for years not wanted to look at her, too scared to know the truth, fearful of her being too much for me to handle. Yet if I didn't, I would still be carrying her along in the shadows, pulling me down, playing out in all my interactions, not living the wholeness of who I truly am.

All of this conversation was going on inside and seemed to happen in a split second.

I would choose now to feel different. She is worthy of receiving more Love. The love I would not deny a friend so why deny Her this same love.

So in that moment I decided.

Naturally, as I chose, my heart opened a little more, letting the woman before me come closer. Invisible barriers gradually softening. She would never be too much for me. I am never too much.

In that moment, a rush of love like no other, like pink candyfloss, overflowed from my heart to surround this distraught woman. I would bring her home to my heart and all would be well.

And the gentle voice affirmed, "Beautiful." "Love her. Remind her what it is to be fully and unconditionally loved. She has been ignored for too long."

And then the most beautiful thing did happen. A merging, a fusion of light, of colour, of emotion and tears, all at once as the love completely encompassed the shadow of the woman. She was changing, morphing, transforming before my eyes. I was beginning to see her beauty, her light return. Like the love gave her warmth and her cheeks and face slowly began to glow. Tears fell down her face and I too felt the wetness of tears fall down my cheeks and drop into my lap. But these were tears, yes of sadness, but also joy, of relief, of something truly beautiful. The sobs came and my body juddered with release as I/we let go of the shame, the judgement, the guilt, the doubt and fear.

Closer and closer she came to me. Rising from my root and womb I felt a heat moving up to my heart, burning away and awakening an inner fire. We were becoming One. This was not too much; she was not too much. She was me and I her. This felt powerful magic, magnificent, we are magnificent. Fear at last vanquished and the warmth of love rose up, expanding my heart in celebration. She returns home and I am whole.

I took a deep breath and sighed out. Gradually, the tears and body shivers began to subside, and a gentle peace descended. Stillness, quiet, serene, tired, limbs relaxed and floppy. No more resisting, fighting myself. Resting now in the arms of the gentle soft One that held us both.

"Come now, you are here with me. You are blessed with my Holy Grace. You are always home in my heart, in Mother's heart beat we are One. Surrender and rest dear One."

At this, I curled up in foetal position, with knees bent towards my chest, to rest knowing a deep rebirth was emerging from within me.

Journal Entry SSG 2022

Facing our shadow seems insurmountable at times. Sometimes we experience a 'Dark Night of the Soul' when loss and death come knocking at our door. This may be an actual death or loss that can be the trigger to old trauma and feelings of grief. Other times it is the dark that lurks within those aspects that we have forgotten or ignored and that are longing to be called home to Love. We are both light and dark and the power of the dark is what often stays in the shadows but has a potency that carries our primal authentic power and light to regenerate us and bring us back to wholeness.

When we are going through challenging times, we can call upon the great Mother of All, the Divine Mother to hold us in her heart of unconditional Love. The soft, gentle voice that came to me when writing, was the Holy Grace of Lady Mother Mary. Her Love is always there holding you, even when you are not aware of her presence consciously.

Shadow Ritual

Light a candle, set your intention for help with your shadow.

Call upon the Holy Grace of Mother Mary and allow her to hold you and guide you in prayer and healing to embrace your shadow with tenderness and Love.

Find your guided meditation on 'Facing your Shadows' on my website. Link can be found at the back of the book under Resources.

Our Shadow's Golden Treasure

What we can find within our shadow is the wonderful golden treasure, the precious gifts and learning, waiting to be discovered. When we keep these parts hidden, they stay in the shadow, still following us around, still running the show, creating self-sabotage, keeping us small and limited.

When we befriend our shadow, heal and embrace with love, something magical begins to happen, as the energy that was once stuck is liberated and set free.

When we release stuck energy, we also release the life force bound with it, so our vitality increases, we have a sense of completion, of coming home to self and ancient soul gifts are returned to us.

Retrieving the Power of My Voice

I remember this with my voice when I unlocked a part of me that had been shut away, that was too fearful to come out.

On a shamanic journey I was taken down a dark passageway where I found a boulder over a cave. Was I ready to reveal what was behind? Initial fear and resistance came up and then something moved through me and a Yes rose up within me. I was ready.

Magically the boulder rolled over to reveal in the entrances a huge Grandmother Spider. At first, she seemed frightening and then I soon realised she was there protecting something or someone. She moved to one side. There I saw deep in the cave, a young woman and recognised there was something wrong, there was silence – no sound coming from her mouth.

It was then I was taken back in time. Faint memories flickered through my mind. A time where my gut feeling told me she had been persecuted for speaking her truth. Burning witches came to mind, as many of us have been in previous lives. I could understand why she was so scared to share her voice and how that translated into my current life.

Back in the cave, the Spider came and injected into the young woman. Shocked, but quickly realising the nurturing mother spider was awakening something dormant in the young woman. Beautifully I could see floating from her throat and higher heart, rainbow colours of blues, white, pink and gentle sounds began to rise up from her. Tuning into my body at the same time I could feel the shifts starting to take place. I began coughing as my own voice and throat was clearing.

I was then guided to allow the young woman to step free. It was now time to allow the spirit of her essence that had been kept safe, to return to my heart. To embrace her fully.

After the session, it took several months to fully process and integrate these deep changes.

Over the years, there have been further times when I had to revisit my throat. It has been a deep awakening journey. A therapist I saw back in 2020, helped me reclaim the final key to releasing my voice and Soul's song. It was a profound opening and since, I have had the joy of channelling Light Language, chanting, toning and singing my Soul's song, activating the remembering of our Divine right to speak and be heard.

Healing the many lifetimes and spirals, I am eventually overcoming the blocks to self-expression and setting my voice free. This is my soul's journey which I am truly grateful for. I feel more confident to express my views, to show up and be more visible and I love to share my voice with my sound healing.

What to Do When You Feel Triggered?

When we are first triggered, we are often in the raw emotion of it. It will probably feel difficult at this point to detach and observe. At best, if you are communicating with someone directly when this happens, do your best to express how you feel without attacking or blaming. If necessary, remove yourself from the situation so you don't say something that you might regret later but give yourself the option to come back when you have calmed down.

Expressing emotions is a good thing. It can discharge a situation and relationships built on honesty, clears any resentment or tension that may be in the air.

When you are on your own and can give yourself quality time and care, settle yourself down to connect with yourself.

Take some long deep breaths to slow everything down. When ready, say 'hello' and acknowledge the feelings and thoughts that are surfacing. Write them down if this helps.

Allow yourself to feel what you feel, whether it is expressing tears, hurt, anger, sadness or fear.

When you are ready, call upon your Higher Self-wisdom to come in. Align yourself with the overlighting presence of your Soul's wisdom by calling in light and love.

Call upon your spiritual guides, teachers, angels and helpers in the unseen realms to come close.

Lady Mother Mary is one of my beautiful guides. She brings her heart of Grace and Mercy to help us find peace and forgiveness.

Try to observe the emotions, rather than engage in the drama of the feeling and the story of what happened, so that you can begin to see more clearly how the shadow part is operating.

Ask your Higher Self to show you the root cause of this emotional pain.

Often, we re-experience trauma from childhood so give yourself permission to connect with your Inner Child. Mentally communicate with her saying, "I see you...I hear you.... I feel your pain." Hold her in your heart's love. Tell her, "How much I love you..." and repeat this in a soothing, calming, compassionate voice. You can say this out loud or internally. Explore what feels best. You may find yourself gently rocking yourself, as if you are cradling a young child in your arms. Look into the mirror and meet yourself with your own eyes. Sending love and compassion to yourself looking back at you. It may be the young child in you that needs to know she is loved and cared for.

I use this approach myself and with clients. It really helps to develop a loving internal relationship which is the way to rebuild our self-esteem.

Most importantly, come from your heart, from a place of non-judgement for this is a part of YOU. Initially you may find this difficult and so seeking professional support is truly worth- while to help you safely build a loving relationship with yourself.

Often our shadow is the parts and the stories and beliefs that have been passed down from our ancestors, our mothers' and fathers' stories and their grandmothers' and grandfathers'. A different time, a different place but nonetheless they have an impact on our beliefs, on our attitude and behaviours and our health.

Righiful Rage

Anger is often a hidden emotion spilling out, causing frustration and irritation at other people and situations. It is a difficult emotion to process although some people use anger as a way of expressing themselves and masking deep hurt and grief. It's particularly more acceptable for men to express anger and frustration at other things such as road rage.

As women, we often experience frustration and anger when we are pre-menstrual or when we are going through the menopause as previously unresolved issues surface. Over the years I have done a huge amount of shadow work, but anger is probably one of the emotions I find most difficult.

For a woman to express her anger is judged by society as not feminine and doesn't fit in the profile of 'good girl.'

But we can see that the Earth, her true nature, is both peace and calm and wild storms. It is these times of wild winds and seas that we witness her wrath, that can sweep away dense heavy energy making way for clear fresh skies and air. It's just part of her nature. If we take the same view, we can allow our dark emotions to be a way of self-expression, a way of letting go and making space for new clarity.

Rightful rage is when we use anger in a positive way to express our passion but is also our way of protecting ourselves. You perhaps know that feeling when someone has crossed your boundary, well at least your body will tell you. You may have that uncomfortable gut feeling that this is not OK, that your boundaries have been crossed or that you have been violated or abused in some way.

I recall a time myself.

Having grown up with rules and conditions, perhaps once a secure foundation I have most definitely outgrown. I now find them constraining. I want freedom and for all of us to feel safe to freely express ourselves without censorship.

Of course, we need some framework and rules as a guide base to sustain our society, otherwise there could be absolute chaos. Although I do wonder if a natural order would eventually occur, just like Mother Earth needs to keep her balance and equilibrium.

There was a time when I was visiting hospital, certain rules which impacted my ability to speak and express myself. This caused me great distress and a sense of feeling trapped.

This situation triggered me. I felt very upset, challenged as I felt forced into submission. Threatened. On reflection, knowing how I felt, I could have made the choice to leave as a way of honouring and protecting myself. I felt a whole mixture of emotions, fear, shame and humiliation and hurt.

This situation took me on a healing journey. Rather timely, I was meeting with my mentor/coach the next day and when I shared what happened, deep emotion surfaced and tears spilled over. I realised although I was upset about this situation, these emotions came from somewhere else, deep within. I was uncovering another level of emotion relating to all the other times in this life, and past lives, where I had felt marginalised, humiliated, shamed for being different and expressing my truth. I felt great fear of conflict but also what surfaced to my surprise was anger. Anger in this case, for my rights were violated. Now this may have been extreme emotions for this situation, but I was feeling all the lifetimes when my freedom had been squashed.

For many of us we will have experienced past lives where expressing our truth would have threatened our safety and many of us would have been killed for speaking out. We can understand therefore, how difficult it is for many of us to overcome this deep fear.

Allowing my anger and frustration to surface was liberating, as it allowed me to access a deeper sense of my power. Now I can use this anger to create safer boundaries as my body knows clearly now what she is comfortable with and where she draws the line. I then took action to pre-empt my next appointment, taking charge to create a different outcome.

Sometimes we don't know we hold on to anger until we are triggered by someone or a situation. Give thanks to that person or event as this is a gift to help you heal.

Even if we don't have a strong feeling of anger, we may experience smouldering anger just like looming dark clouds in the sky, threatening to explode. We may feel an underlying frustration or irritation that we can't place where it comes from. We don't always need to know the story but what can be helpful is to engage in some cathartic release and feminine embodiment practices. Here are some suggestions...

Letting Go

Movement

If you can get yourself moving. Out in Nature is a wonderful way to feel the elements supporting you.

Like for me, when I could still feel the frustration I was feeling under the surface, I took myself for a walk down to the beach.

Connecting with the wild wind and waves of the sea allowed me to holler out into the wind my frustrations. Making sounds from deep in the gut and belly helped me release. I used my arms and marched down along the shore, feeling the waves whipping at my heels, encouraging me to let go.

On the way back, my frustrations spent, I waded in the shallows of the sea that had left pools of warmer water, now feeling lighter and enjoying the freshness cleansing the soles of my feet. My walking had slowed and except for some large yawning of release, I felt calmer and a joy licking at the edges of my mouth. I began marvelling at the treasures that the sea had washed up, which is something I love to do. I noticed a black smooth stone, flattish and in the gentle curves of a heart. I leant down to pick it up. It felt a perfect fit in my hand. I felt a little token of my journey with anger to take home with me. I thanked the sea for her gift and carried the stone home.

Body Shaking

Body shaking is a wonderful way to get heavy energy moving and releasing.

How does she want to move to express how she feels?

Start by planting your bare feet on the floor or ground. You can do this with music or without.

Begin to move your legs, bouncing gently so your knees are cushioned and supported.

Gradually move up your body, allowing your hips to bounce as if you are springing and pushing your physical body and feet into the ground.

Again, move up to your chest and bring movement to your arms, hands and feet – shaking them whilst keeping your feet planted on the floor to keep you grounded.

Keep bouncing and shaking all the way up your body.

Embodiment Dance

Again, moving your body, but this time I invite you to choose some soundscape that suits your mood.

Do you want a beat and rhythm that your body wishes to move to? Or something inviting softness and flow to help open yourself up?

Tune into your breath first, quietening the mind and tuning into your belly. Anchor your breath in your pelvic bowl. Plant your feet on the ground, feeling the toes gently push down giving you stability.

When you are ready, begin playing the music and turning your gaze inwards. Softly, begin to move your body from the inside out, letting your body be your beautiful guide in how she wishes to express herself. Allow any emotion of sadness or tears to flow or you may find passion rises and you feel such joy as your body moves and your heart opens. Have fun playing and exploring your body and how she wishes to move.

Journal Prompts

1. As you reflect on your shadow, what aspects do you tend to avoid looking at?

2. What unconscious patterns play out in your relationships?

3. What do you notice in others that may be a mirror for what is going on within you?

CHAPTER 15:
Our Ancesıral Lineage and Ancesıral Healing

The stories of our ancestors are carried in our DNA, our blood and bone, and so like our forefathers and the women who came before us, we carry the same genes that make up our physical traits as wells as our beliefs, patterns, and emotions. This comes down our umbilical cord at birth.

There is a lot of strength and wisdom to be gained by learning our ancestral history. Understanding their lives, the challenges they would have had to face, and how they overcame them or not.

Researching Your Ancesıors

Were they involved in any of the major world wars and how this is likely to have contributed to their beliefs around money, scarcity thinking, and so on?

Women may have been strong in your family but what of their need to show vulnerability and ask for support?

On the father side, what was their work and to what extent did they struggle and strive to feed and provide for the family?

Often there is shame on both sides that can have undercurrents for ourselves.

These qualities, strengths and weaknesses greatly influence our lives, as the energetic imprints and undercurrents play out, often unconsciously, initially.

Ancesıral Healing

Ancestral healing has been an important part of my own healing journey.

As souls, we often incarnate together in families with the purpose of helping to clear and heal certain limiting patterns and frequencies that have been stuck in our lineage. We can break the energetic chain and create freedom not just for ourselves, but we also liberate the souls of our mother/father lineage and for our future generations.

A female client I worked with once came to me wanting to understand the reasons why she couldn't make enough money in her business. We journeyed inwards a few times to discover the root of the issue. Together we discovered a few lifetimes down her father side of poverty, of gambling and low self-esteem. Money is another form of currency and therefore energy – it is like seeing water running away down a plug hole – a sense that our own life force is draining away. In the journeys we understood the cause, sought forgiveness, and brought through love and healing to dissolve trauma and to rewrite with new beliefs. Doing this at a deep unconscious level allows the patterns to shift. We also did another journey to address her self-esteem and to come into balance with her feminine and masculine, which strengthened her confidence. It has been wonderful to see how she is now creating new ways of working that are more aligned with her values, that creates abundance not just for herself but others.

We all incarnate with a key wound or pattern and for many of us on the spiritual path, wake up to the realisation that these can be healed. My guess if you are reading this, you are curious about your ancestral lineage and how it is influencing your life choices.

Like the pattern of judgement and self-judgement that I came in to experience and heal. This is one of our family patterns which I feel comes from our father side, that has affected our self-esteem and self-worth. I believe it is a collective issue for our generation. Linked to this is the wound of betrayal which creates a pattern of mistrust and self-denial.

On our mother side there are all the women whose voices were never heard, a lack of power and self-worth of not feeling valued or having an empowered place in society. Their sexual life force was tamed and suppressed, so no wonder we have so many hang-ups about our body and self-image and distortions around our sexuality.

Again, these are all generational issues that we are now facing as a collective to heal. Our ancestors would not have had the resources, time, money, nor the skill set or awareness to express and heal their traumas and emotions. It is different for us today as mental health and expressing our emotions is becoming much more acceptable. We are on a new timeline to rebalance the feminine and masculine and bring unity and peace to the world.

Our Core Wounds

~Betrayal

~Abandonment and Rejection

~Judgement

~Denial

Betrayal – how we may have been betrayed by another and in turn have taken on that experience and betray our own sense of self and truth.

Abandonment – a key wound often found in childhood and often found in the root chakra of our being. The root chakra is the foundation of life where we either feel secure or insecure and influences how much we feel safe and secure in the world.

Judgement – judgemental patterns can influence our level of self-esteem through negative self-talk. Having been brought up in an environment where we are criticised as a way of bettering yourself to become perfect. The opposite to self-acceptance.

Denial – denying what we feel, saying 'yes' when we mean 'no' is a fundamental denial of our own truth. People pleasing falls under this category.

Spend time reflecting and researching your immediate ancestors and see what patterns start to come to light that you can also see running in your own life.

If resources were limited, then imagine what their lives might have been, what challenges they would have had to face and what impact that may have had on their perception of life.

Turning Grief into Gratitude

Through forgiveness and healing, we can alchemise our wounds into gifts of wisdom, surrender and enlightenment. This is the journey home to our true authentic self.

Betrayal becomes **Trust** in oneself and in Love, to trust the flow of Life and the wisdom of our heart to guide us safely.

Abandonment becomes **Self-Love** and **Oneness** – surrendering to something greater than ourselves knowing we are part of the whole.

Judgement becomes **Forgiveness** which brings Peace to us and the world.

Denial becomes **Truth** – allowing our truth to be spoken with love and compassion and without apology.

Healing Our Lineage

Ancestral Dolls

Healing our ancestral patterns starts with becoming more self-aware. Notice what repeating patterns and emotions you are experiencing. You can then consciously start working with the intention to heal and transform these wounds.

I remember a time when I was healing my ancestral lineage and I was out walking in our local woods, contemplating my father's life and history, when a long, rotting stick poked out from a bush causing me to stop in my tracks. It called to me as symbolic of the self- judgement that my father and his father had carried and never expressed, causing repressed tension and hidden depression. I took the stick to bring back to my sacred space, to work with.

Another time I gathered some natural material to make an ancestral doll that would represent my mother line and my daughter. I dressed them in cut off pieces of cloth that I had kept aside in a little box. I found a brown, shiny conker that represented the wisdom and nourishment she carried on her back and a shell resembling a turban for her headdress.

It is wonderful to work in this way, as it brings to life the qualities of what you imagine your lineage has passed down to you, as well as aspects that still need healing.

I worked with both in ceremony, at Samhain to honour my ancestors. And through the weeks that followed they sat in my sacred space. When it came to the Winter Solstice, I felt guided to take them to my local woods and bury them. In this act I felt I was gifting to the Earth Mother for healing, returning to the earth all that was ready to be released, let go of. It was a very moving experience burying, laying to rest, surrendering to the Great Mother to compost them, to create space for renewal in the light of the Solstice new dawn.

You can create your own ways to honour and work with your ancestors.

You may like to create something in honour of them such as painting, creating ancestor dolls or working with something from Nature that represents what you are healing or letting go of. Or perhaps the wisdom and strength you want to remember them by.

Unravelling to Remember

Unravelling the stories that kept us tame

Unravelling the judgement and shame

Setting us free to remember

The beauty of our heart and soul

The magic of Life that holds us

Returning us home to wholeness.

My ancestors stand close by.

I honour their wisdom and strength

that flows to me now.

Journal Entry - Death Circle, Samhain, Red Tent Circle of Women

As I sit in the powerful circle of women, I listen to each woman share her story of death and loss and I am touched by how she has been affected. My heart goes out to each woman as she bravely shares her story. Some cry, some find it difficult to give voice to what they feel but shakily they do as the other women express their compassion, giving strength and courage for them to continue.

And then it is my turn. I hold the talking stick. I know not what to say, my mind blank, so I pause to be still and connect with my heart to see what wants to rise. Immediately, I feel immense love as my ancestors come close, to hold me. I take a deep breath as my heart expands, not knowing whether I am going to cry from the feelings of immense love. I realise now that my dad is here, his love fully present in my heart. I begin to speak about when my dad died many years ago on 30 October 2011. I recall how intense it was as he died within a week of being diagnosed with a rare form of aggressive cancer.

Through tears, I retell the story of his passing and how I had the privilege of helping his soul cross into the light. I struggle to speak, as emotions bubble up and nearly overwhelm me.

Then take a breath and recognise I want to declare the pattern of betrayal and blame that I believe has come down my father's lineage. I don't know the story of what had happened, but I am familiar with the pattern of self-blame and of guilt that has permeated our family. In the witness of this women's circle, words flowed from my mouth, "I choose to release and let go so that my ancestors and I are free." It feels powerful to say this, as although I have grieved for my father many years ago, echoes of this betrayal pattern still cling, and I am ready to let it all go.

Journal Entry SSG 2019

The power of witness is not to be underestimated. In the days that followed, I was aware of processing the emotions that came up that evening in circle. I was also acutely aware of the lack of mothering I had as a child and the grief of not having enough love and the effect this had on my self-esteem. Like many others of our generation, our mothers and fathers didn't know how to express their love because they too didn't experience the love they needed to flourish. And therefore, the absence of love gets passed down through the generations.

For now, I find peace in allowing another layer of grief and loss to drop away. I give myself space to be nothing other than what I feel in this moment.

Interestingly, later in the autumn and winter months, my mother became very ill and spent eight weeks in hospital. This was a deeply healing experience for me and my sisters. At this stage of my mother's life, she held what is known in shamanic terms as the 'karmic torch,' highlighting the sisterly dynamics between us and our relationship with mother and what still needed to be healed and forgiven. It was during this challenging time of travelling long distance to visit my mum, that I found my heart cracked open even wider. I realised I had held resistance to receiving her love as I was still holding onto pain in my heart from childhood that kept my heart not fully open to her.

Seeing my mum so vulnerable, my heart just cracked open so wide with compassion, I realised how much I loved her and told her so. Tears flowed for us both. It was in these moments of bravely sharing my heart's love, that I was able to also receive her love, to quench the thirst that my inner child so needed to find peace with the feelings of 'not good enough.' Gratefully, this facilitated a deeper connection between us.

Here is another woman's story of her relationship with her mother and how through a shamanic healing journey we were able to facilitate a shift in perception that would instigate the beginning of more positive connection for them both.

A Woman's Story - 'The Owl and The Ancesiors'

The path to healing is a winding road but one that I have traversed intrepidly. Despite it appearing that I have backtracked or regressed at times, this has never been the case due to what I now understand to be an upwardly increasing spiral of greater wisdom and insight. I consistently come back around to the same healing themes but from different elevated angles, in ways that allow me to understand with deeper clarity, compassion and acceptance. I would like to tell you about one such healing journey that I found to be especially poignant and profound.

At the beginning of 2021, I discovered that I was carrying a new life within my womb. This was unexpected and an enormous blessing at a time in life when my body's rhythms had begun to show signs that its days of fertility were numbered. As time progressed, I was delighted to discover that I was carrying a baby girl. Those nine months were an intense period of gratitude and deep rest. It was also a time of the letting go of a sense of normality both in my own life, as well as in the wider society that was changed forever by the advent of the Covid pandemic.

Carrying my first daughter, I became increasingly aware of my mother wound – of estrangement, pain, and trauma – more fully perceiving the imbalance of femininity and female expression that I had co-created in this lifetime. There were so many whispered hopes and prayers for this new life swelling and blossoming within, but there were also fears. I held and caressed my growing abdomen silently speaking to my daughter, promising that I would love her without compromise, that I would do everything within my power not to repeat history, and that I would continue to heal the wounds of the past so that they were not passed on to her.

Then miraculously, about six months into the pregnancy, I heard from my mother for the first time in about twenty years. My initial reaction was of fear and an enormous protective instinct for my wellbeing and that of my family. I didn't write back straight away. After the initial shock of this letter out of the blue, I leaned into the possibility of hope for reconnecting with my mother and of the potential for healing the ancestral female lineage. I took a deep breath and wrote back to her, starting the journey of slowly repairing this most painful of broken relationships.

Over the years, I have felt intrinsically linked with my mother. Even throughout our estrangement I intuited when she moved overseas, and now know that I was correct in my sensing of that physical shift. Despite my effort to clear and heal the energies and cords between us, I also felt when she was not in a good state of mind. The mother/child bond goes far deeper than just love, genetics, or familiarity. Known only in the depth of our souls, I feel that for better or worse, we choose to be born through our mothers for specific reasons. Even when physically apart, it is difficult to comprehend the enormity and complexity of the energetic and psychic merging we experience with our mothers.

Towards the end of my pregnancy, I was offered a remote healing journey by Sonraya which I graciously accepted. In explaining my reasons for needing to dive more deeply into healing the feminine wound, she guided me on an inner journey with the aim of finding out whether any further healing could take place – specially to clear the way for my daughter to feel safe and ready to be born through me and into my family lineage.

After the meditation induction and deep relaxation, I found myself looking upon the vision of a past life where I was dressed simply in a tunic style dress, living in what looked like a mud hut with a fire stove. I was looking out on my life as a young mother, watching my daughter play and help to attend to the daily chores. But this peaceful and happy vision was short-lived because some strange men came along and took her away. I was alone and despite my best attempts, I was physically unable to prevent the abduction. I felt distraught and heartbroken that I was unable to protect my daughter from the pain and terror of that experience. She survived and returned to me in that lifetime but was forever changed and affected by what had happened – her innocence lost and the trust gone.

Whilst witnessing that experience remotely, it became clear that the daughter in my meditation was the same soul who is now my mother. In this current life, even with our familial roles reversed, I have been similarly unable to protect her from the pain, abuse and trauma she experienced before I was even born to her this time around. This new-found awareness goes a long way to explain why I have felt so responsible for attempting to help my mother with her pain this lifetime, and why I have felt guilt for not being able to heal her heart more fully.

One of the hardest things I've learnt is that despite my best intentions, I cannot help to undo what has been done or facilitate healing in someone if they are unwilling or not ready to take responsibility for their own pain and healing journey. Regardless of the parts we play in one another's lives, we are each responsible for our own physical, mental, emotional and spiritual wellbeing.

Sonraya closed the healing journey by guiding me back to the present to sit around a campfire with the soul family from the vision. However, it felt as if all the ancestors were with us, holding space and witnessing the shift. We sat in still knowing, silently acknowledging the parts we played and continue to play in our interwoven lives. We sat in acceptance, forgiveness, and compassion for what we had witnessed, seeing it from the higher wisdom-filled perspective of our soul's birds eye view. As we sat, a large owl flew down into the circle with a loose feather floating down from its wings to land on each of our laps – a parting gift of the wisdom that we could each take away from the experience. I left Sonraya's healing session with an immense sense of peace, and with a strong thread of love for my feminine lineage that knows no end.

I have since come to a deep inner knowing that when something feels like an enormous weight to carry in life, we must exercise great patience to allow grace to work through us. Most of us are consciously unaware of the intricate tapestries of many lifetimes lived, and of the unpicking of karmic knots that if left unattended cause dis-harmony, dis-ease, and dis-chord. However, with an open mind and heart, we get opportunities to glimpse into our deeper spiritual truths and do the shadow work necessary to allow our souls to take flight.

A deeply auspicious sign came to me not long after Sonraya's healing session. It was nearing midnight on a still and quiet starry night. Whilst in the throes of a strong contraction en route to the labour ward, an owl swooped down flying parallel to the window on my passenger side of the car for what seemed like a considerable time, before crossing over in front of the windscreen and up and away into the trees. Phenomenally, it was the same species of owl from the vision around the campfire. I was filled with a Divine sense of peace and reverence in that moment – so much so that my labour pains abated a little for the remainder of the journey.

My daughter was born safely and peacefully into the world not long after this deeply transformative and healing series of events. It feels like a profound gift to us both that we were able to energetically witness a clearing of some of the more challenging aspects of the mother/feminine dynamic before her arrival Earth-side. And despite any inner work and healing that undoubtedly still needs to be undertaken, my daughter still consciously chose to be born through me, for which I hold an un-ending gratitude. I also continue to work on reconnecting and healing the bond with my own mother this lifetime, which feels less cluttered by heaviness every time a giant leap forward like this takes place.

Each and every day I practice radical acceptance of the things I find challenging but cannot change. I practice radical compassion for the pain and trauma I continue to work on resolving. I practice radical gratitude for the whole journey – the good as well as the perceived bad – which provides me with more opportunities for growth and improvement. And piece by piece, I learn radical forgiveness of myself for my part in this great story that unfolds more profoundly through lifetimes lived, beautifully interwoven in between the lives of loved ones loved.

Tanya

Journal Prompts

1. What do you know about your ancestors on your mother side?

2. What do you know about your ancestors on your father side?

3. What traits do you feel you carry from each lineage? Focus on both the positive and aspects that you would like to heal?

4. Can you identify with any of the key wounds mentioned here? How do they play out in your life? What impact do they have on your self-esteem, health and wellbeing, sense of wealth?

5. What aspects would you like to address and resolve?

6. With every wound there is a gift waiting to be released. What do you imagine this to be, the flipside?

Vulnerability – Our Tender Selves

Feeling vulnerable and sharing our vulnerability are two different things.

As a child I would run to my room to cry because there was no space for emotions in our household. I had learnt to keep them hidden, as it didn't feel safe to express them.

My mum felt the burden of caring for three daughters and a husband that worked day and night. Little space for visible love or nourishment grew here. Suppression and control were the dominant features and being a sensitive heart star, I took this all in and made it about me. That's not to say that love did not exist, because it did, but as a young child I did not feel it was there, as it was never overtly expressed.

So, it became a habit to hold on, doing what I could to get by, to keep safe, but feeling sad that I didn't feel able to fully express myself or have a mother who was present with love in her heart to share and nourish me. I know she carried a deep sadness too, as she never received the loving and nurturing she so desperately needed and so the wheel kept turning through the generations.

Mother Nature was my source of joy. I recall as a baby being put in one of those old-fashioned prams in the garden with warm sunlight listening to the birds. Nature and the birds became my friends, the winged messengers who have been with me all my life.

Journal Entry – Tenderness

Yesterday I revisited those places of pain I had held in my body, another level of the spiral of healing, and merging and surrendering with my soul and spirit.

As my chiropractor placed her fingers on various parts of my body, I found my body began to move and unlock and suddenly a release was inevitable. A tidal wave of sobs rose from deep down within, a scream of what was not heard or witnessed before, of sadness, of grief, of deep sorrow. The sounds from my body were familiar to a baby's scream and yet there were other sounds and voices taking the opportunity to release through me too; old ones distorted through the generations of my mother and the women who came before her and from my previous lives that had kept me bound.

I lay for a while as my body's sobs gradually subsided, feeling the magnitude of what I had expressed.

As I came round and sat up, I slowly opened my eyes to see my chiropractor's warm loving eyes looking back at me, honouring my surrender and all that I had moved through.

Today I feel fragile, yet strangely OK. I realise as I look back, I have always been held by Life itself and I can allow myself to feel that, deeper in my blood and bones than ever before. I am grateful for being alive to experience emotions, for without them I wouldn't know joy.

I share me as I AM! I have taken another step of opening up to Life so that it can flow through me. I love myself unconditionally as I am.

Journal Entry SSG 2018

We all need holding and being witnessed at times, celebrating the important and significant moments of growth in our lives.

Whatever breakthroughs and breakdowns you are having or have had, allow yourself to feel tender and vulnerable, for in this place we truly come to know who we are. We realise in the crumbling and falling away, we allow Life's love to enter, to crack open our heart, revealing the raw, beautiful, and pure me.

Allow yourself to feel safe in your body and be held by Mother Earth and your guides. Reach out and ask for support. Find a safe space with a friend, with your tribe or sisterhood, with a professional therapist.

Go out into Nature. Plant your feet deep into Mamma Earth, stand with your back to the trunk of a tree and feel its strength fill your spine and nervous system. Let it all go. Allow your cries and sounds to be heard on the wind, or to be heard by another, to be witnessed supported and loved. There is something very special when we are witnessed or when we can witness another in their time of most need.

Give love to those parts of you that may still be holding on. Let her know it's safe to show herself, that she is loved, adored and cherished, even if her upbringing was not as she would have wanted.

Daily Mantra

I TRUST I AM enough just as I AM.

I am perfect.

I love myself unconditionally.

Healing My Shadow Exercises

Here are some exercises to support your Shadow healing. Guided meditations can be found on my website.

Exercise 1 – The Golden Chair

Create a quiet space for you to meditate.

Set the space and intention for your time with yourself.

Light a candle in dedication.

- Relax and breathe.
- You may like to first focus on the candle flame, noticing its light and warmth and flickering presence. When you feel relaxed, gently close your eyes.
- Ground your body, breathing deep down into your pelvic bowl, your legs and feet.
- Feel your roots go deep down into the heart of Mother Earth. Feel her hold you steady. Breathe her love up into your womb and then into your heart.
- Imagine you are sitting on a seat in a beautiful garden. Sunshine is shining down upon you and the seat. You are enveloped in a warm glow.
- Bring to attention an aspect of you that feels uncomfortable, or that you don't like.
- Invite this part of you that may be feeling hurt or fearful, to come forward and sit next to you. It may be a younger version of yourself.
- Ask: How old are they? It is easier to see or sense this part outside of yourself first.
- Listen to this other part. What does she want to share with you? What doubts, emotions and feelings does she have? Listen as you would to a friend sitting next to you, without judgement and with compassion.
- Keep listening with all your senses.
- Connect with your Higher Self, the light and infinite source of wisdom. You may like to imagine this as pure golden light coming through the crown of your head and coming into your heart, softening, and expanding it. Feel your heart relax and open. Breathe in this light and love.
- Send a stream of love from your heart to the part of you sitting on the seat next to you. Imagine they are in front of your heart receiving this flow of love. How does it feel as you both connect? Breathe into the feeling and this connection.
- What is the lesson? What is the gift in this situation?

- When you are ready and if this feels right for you at this time, invite this other part of you to come forward and into your heart to merge with you.
- Sit for a while, feeling this integration happening on an energetic level. You may like to place your hand on your heart, in loving presence, sealing this reunion, of this part of yourself. Welcome the lost part of you, home.

When you invite this part of you into the alchemical pot of your heart, it evokes the process of glorious transformation. Something magical begins to happen. Something new and different becomes possible. The love of your heart is alchemy in motion.

Be aware that you may experience more of the emotions as they surface in your heart.

Just as base metal turns into gold, we find the golden treasure within the shadow, and we realise we are already whole.

Love transcends shadow, the shadow becomes part of the light, and the light becomes part of the shadow. The shadow is seen, it is no longer travelling behind you but is part of you, and is you, warts, and all.

Love yourself just as you are.

Miracles do happen as you embrace, love, and accept yourself. That's the simplicity of it.

That's the truth.

You can find a Guided Meditation – Healing My Inner Child – links at the back of the book under Resources - that will safely and lovingly guide you to heal emotional pain and begin building a new loving relationship with yourself.

When to Get Professional Help?

Sometimes the pain is so deep and overwhelming we need to seek support from someone skilled and professional who can hold the space safely for us. There is no shame in asking for support. In fact, often it is a wise choice to ask for help.

As you are held in a safe container, so you can go to a deeper place, discovering the root cause that you may have been blind to. In my own journeys in the past, I have been taken many times deep into my subconscious to connect with parts of myself that I have forgotten. This is what we call 'soul loss or fragmentation.' Often hidden in a cave or locked away in our psyche, with help we are able to overcome the obstacles to reach those parts with love and compassion. Often there is a process of forgiveness required and then these parts are brought home to our heart for integration into wholeness.

Because of the level of experience and my heightened self-awareness through years of personal development work, I am able to do this more often now for myself. But there are still times when I like to be held in a safe supportive space, to let go and receive. Keeping the balance of giving and receiving, however experienced we are, is so important to keeping in flow and harmony.

Exercise 2 – Hawaiian Ho'oponopono Prayer

There are other techniques I use to bring healing to emotional situations, including the Hawaiian Prayer.

This is an especially powerful exercise when done with heartfelt connection and intent. It has the power to shift the spiralling thoughts and bring healing and peaceful resolution to our relationships.

Hawaiian Ho'oponopono Prayer

I am sorry.....

Please forgive me ......

Thank you......

I love you........

With clear intent and meaning, this is a powerful exercise to shift energy and open the heart. It is best repeated a few times and regularly if you are having difficulties with a person or you feel a part of yourself has become alienated and you wish to heal and integrate into wholeness.

Preparation

Set aside a quiet space where you won't be disturbed. You may even wish to light a candle in dedication to bringing healing and resolution to this situation.

Imagine the person/yourself or situation in front of you. If it's a pain in the body, focus and hold the area of pain with your hand, if this is possible.

Breathe through your mouth. Feel the essence of the following words as you repeat each. Do this slowly and with care. Repeat three times.

I am sorry

This does not mean you have done anything wrong just that you are sorry that this situation has come about. You are acknowledging the pain and discomfort that this situation has created for both of you.

Please forgive me

Holding on to anger and resentment only hurts and damages you as well as anyone you love, as it can cause the heart to close and not fully open to all people and situations. Forgiving does not mean what happened, what was said or done is OK, but you are giving the situation and yourself the love and compassion you need, to let it go. This helps you to be free to move forwards into your future.

Thank you

Regardless of what may or may not have happened, there are always lessons to be learnt about our self. Everything is a mirror teaching us to go deeper into compassion and self-acceptance that aids the further growth of our Soul. Each person that crosses our path offers a gift.

Sometimes these gifts are uncomfortable as we need to look deeper into our own hurts and traumas that may be being triggered by this person or situation. When we say thank you, we take responsibility for the choices we have made, letting go of judgement and especially any self-judgement in the process.

I love you

Saying, 'I love you,' brings the heart energy of love to the situation and importantly to yourself. Love transcends fear and takes us back to our original source and connection to Oneness.

As you repeat these words either in your head or out loud, notice what sensations and feelings this evokes within your heart and body.

Forgiveness Prayer

All those things in the past

That you judge yourself for

The mistakes, the things said and done, you regret

That arrow of pain in your heart

Let them go now, my love

This pain, this burden you carry, for what purpose does it serve you to hold?

A burden too heavy to bear that keeps you bound

Let go, surrender to my Holy Love

Forgive yourself for past misdeeds for in the wholeness of Life

All is accepted and absorbed by my Love

Feel my love carry you beyond your fears and doubts

Let my Love erase and dissolve all transgressions

Forgive those that have trespassed against you and all those you have
trespassed against

Forgive yourself first for it is not until we completely honour and love ourselves
Unconditionally, can we forgive and accept another

Allow the magnificence of your Divine Love to carry all

Feel my Holy Love bathe you in Light

'A rainbow shower of golden light falling upon my crown'

All is forgiven, I judge you not

Let Love's peace find its way deep into your heart

'Pain softening, relaxing gone'

I surrender

I am peace.

Lady Mother Mary, spoken through Sonraya Grace

CHAPTER 16:

Allowing Space to Grieve

Permission to Grieve

In the cycles and seasons of the Earth, there is a natural phase for grieving.

During Autumn and Winter, leaves naturally fall and all becomes bare. This is a valuable time to draw the curtains on the outer world and go within to nurture our inner world. Here we let go, and peel back the layers of our ego and all that is no longer beneficial to carry. We experience grief as old emotions surface for healing and resolution.

Being witnessed in our grieving is a very powerful healing process that may be done professionally on an individual basis or in a group.

Understanding What Grief is

The medical definition of grief is:

The normal process of reacting to a loss. The loss may be physical (such as a death), social (such as a divorce) or occupational (such as a job). Emotional reactions of grief can include, anger, guilt, anxiety, sadness and despair, hopelessness and numbness. You may have experienced other emotions and of course we all experience grief and the experience of loss differently, due to our own personal history and personality.

Firstly, it is important to recognise that grief is a natural part of change. Grief comes from a sense of loss, whether that is from the death of a family member, loved one, friend, colleague or family pet or from a physical loss or social loss. It can affect us in many ways and sometimes we are not conscious of the true impact it has on us. There is often an expectation we place upon ourselves that once a funeral has passed that the grieving is over.

Environmental circumstances sometimes make it difficult for us to grieve fully. For example, being a mother with young children, one may expect to give priority of care to the children, putting our own grief on hold. However, in the long run, gone unchecked, this can cause mental and emotional health problems further down the line and a disconnection with our true self.

This can also occur when we are young. Our social and parental upbringing can have a significant and detrimental effect on our level of self-esteem. Such as a sense of loss of innocence, self-worth, confidence, and feelings of shame. An event in adulthood may trigger the underlying feelings of grief we experienced in childhood. This often happens when we give birth to our own children.

Becoming a mother, we naturally revisit our experience of childhood and how we were parented. Any unresolved grief or loss we experienced that was not fully processed at the time is likely to come up for healing and resolution. This grief is often a contributory factor to those with post-natal depression. Seeking professional support and addressing this early is fundamental for our health and wellbeing. It is nothing to be ashamed of. As new mums, we are usually feeling very vulnerable and emotional due to hormones and lack of sleep. Asking practical help from family and friends, perhaps with food shopping, meal preparation and other household jobs can greatly help, as well as a good friend or social care worker can lead a valuable listening ear. If we don't address these feelings, they can stay locked in the cells and organs of our body contributing to physical symptoms and disease.

Everyone's grief process is unique.

Being a witness to our own grief and that of another is a true gift of listening and receiving.

Five Key Stages of Grief

The five stages of grief were first developed by Elizabeth Kubler-Ross in her book On *Death and Dying* in 1969 and since then many health professionals refer to it as a useful model for helping people understand and process grief. She subsequently wrote and co-authored with David Kessler her second book in 2005, *Grief and Grieving*, unfortunately whilst on her death bed.

The cycle of grief is known to cover five phases, although this is not necessarily experienced in a linear fashion. You may experience some but not all and may loop back and forth just like we experience a spiral.

Denial – Anger – Bargaining – Depression – Acceptance

Denial – shock, inability to face the reality. Helps us to pace ourselves so that we can handle as much as we can at one time.

Anger – looking to blame others, self, guilt – lashing out at others.

Bargaining – The 'What if …' stage. Trying to bargain, say with a higher power, God, Universe, to put off the inevitable.

Depression – depression when reality sinks in, intense sadness, loss of motivation and appetite, not wanting to get up in the morning, hiding away from social contact.

Acceptance – there is more acceptance and recognition of the loss. It doesn't necessarily mean that your grief is complete, you may have good and bad days. It's a gradual process.

One of the myths of the grieving process is that we only experience emotions. As our emotions impact our physical body, we can experience physical symptoms such as sleeplessness, nightmares, extreme tiredness, stress, and tension which contribute to bodily aches and pain, loss of appetite, panic attacks, crying and feelings of social isolation.

The Grief Cycle

Grief can also come when there is a sense of loss of self. Perhaps a loss that comes from having a chronic health condition that means you feel you have lost out in life. There are many women who have had to have a hysterectomy where the womb and sometimes the ovaries are removed, or they are unable to have and give birth to children or have had miscarriages or stillbirth. These naturally give rise to a sense of great loss, a loss of their womb, fertility, sense of woman and motherhood and their ability to give birth to children or have any more children.

I remember a lovely woman who came to several of my Retreat days where we were deepening our connection to our wombs. Due to severe health issues, she'd had a hysterectomy, and so hadn't been able to conceive or give birth. Through adoption she was a mum to two beautiful children, and she and her husband were very happy and proud of them. However, old feelings of loss and grief around not being able to conceive and give birth surfaced. We were able to hold her in a loving and safe space, so that her grief could at last be acknowledged and witnessed. This gave space for healing and later resolution through the process of self-forgiveness and acceptance.

So many times, I hear women feeling they had no choice but to have a hysterectomy and hold shame for the choice they made. It is important to develop an attitude of loving kindness and compassion towards ourselves. We make the best decision possible at the time with all the information we have.

Plus, it is important to be aware that although we may not have a physical womb, we still carry the etheric energy of the womb and all its creative potential – the power to tune in and flow with the moon cycles to manifest and give birth to our ideas. We are no less a woman but there may be a process of grieving. A sacred ceremony is a wonderful way to honour, to forgive and come to a place of inner peace and acceptance.

If you are considering a hysterectomy, then I suggest tuning into your womb.

What is she telling you? What unresolved issues and emotions may reside here?

Once you begin to consciously work with your emotions and give space for feelings to surface, then it may be possible for your body to heal itself without intervention. If you still choose to have a hysterectomy then you can still honour your womb through sacred ceremony, giving thanks for all that She has given you and that you now choose to let go of the pain.

Our womb space carries a huge amount of energy and potential but over millennia, women have learnt to suppress their true power, their sense of worth and value, their sensual and sexual nature because of social upbringing. Sadly, the dishonour of the feminine and the Earth has had a powerful impact on the feminine psyche and collective. Women are unlearning what they have been told about themselves and their bodies. This takes time, patience and a whole lot of love, healing, and compassion for oneself.

Loving and self-acceptance is an important part of the grieving process. We talk about womb wisdom and our feminine power in Part One. On my website you can access resources for a Womb and Heart Meditation, a link can be found at the back of the book under Resources.

The loss of a child, a parent or loss of a limb, or quality of life through a chronic illness will require space for grieving, like when I was diagnosed with diabetes in 2001. When women move through different life stages, we experience powerful Rites of Passage. There can be a grieving process, particularly as we move from child to becoming a woman, to motherhood through to the end of our childbearing days, the perimenopause, and the post menopause years as we move into our Crone and elder years.

How You Can Support Yourself During the Grieving Process

- Professional help

  Get professional help to be held and to work through and understand your grief.

- Kindness

  Be kind and loving to yourself. Let go of expectations of how you should feel.

- Body shake

  Shaking your body allows you to release heavy energy and to shift your mood.

- Dance

  Put on your favourite music and move your body. Lose yourself in the rhythm, helping you express difficult emotions like anger or shift feelings of stuckness. Let your heart open to allow emotions to be expressed.

- Patience

  Be patient with yourself, it takes time and self-love.

- Grounding

  Being out in Nature communing with Mother Nature, her beauty and at this time of year notice the falling leaves and her sense of withdrawing her life force. Feel her support you as you let go too. See the beauty in the dying.

- Death Café resources

  These are becoming a popular way to connect with others and explore the meaning of death.

- Compassion

  Holding yourself with compassion and loving acceptance.

- Grief counselling

- Shamanic medicine

A person's death may trigger old childhood feelings and emotions. Shamanic Healing is a powerful way to get to the root of the issue and to begin a life-changing process.

- Red Tent

A sacred space for women to connect and gather. You can search the Internet for your local Red Tent and Death Cafés.

Journal Entry - 'Grieving with Autumn/Fall'

My walk takes me through the damp wooded Chine down to the sea. Her Autumn cloak of different shades of red, browns and yellows create a damp carpet whilst a few remaining leaves tentatively cling to bare branches. The pulse of life is slowing down, as Mother Earth turns inwards ready to sleep.

I am met by the caw of Crow, perched high in a tree, with black iridescent feathers that catch the sun rays breaking through the bare branches. I acknowledge Crow's magical presence.

Suddenly, to my surprise, it flies immediately towards me and just above my head, feeling the movement of air above my crown as it flies past. I feel such awe and excitement as my heart expands in gratitude.

Crows are messengers of spirit and I feel they carry the magic of the void. They are more present in my awareness at this time of year and their guidance is welcomed as we seek to navigate the darkness within.

As I continue my walk down the Chine, the crow flies back to land in front of me on the ground. It is clearly telling me to stop, pause and take in my surroundings. I stop and listen.

My breathing deepens and I close my eyes. I can feel myself merging with the trees, the Earth and the gentle sound of birdsong around. In between the soft sounds of Nature's song, I feel the silence and the heartbeat of creation. It is tangible and magical. I take another deep breath to let this moment sink deeper into my consciousness. I feel this is the message of Crow. To pause and be still. To listen and to open to the magic of Winter.

I give my thanks and eventually begin to carry on my walk, slowly, towards the sea.

As I turn the corner, the sound of the waves greets me. I walk along the water's edge, now feeling the power and love of Mother Sea.

I feel the urge to sit on a bench with sun on my face and I take my journal and pen out from my bag and begin to write. The days after Samhain I am aware of what has been dying in my being – the old ways, the fears and self-judgement and the need to honour the emotions that come with that.

Now feeling soothed by the motion of waves, I find my pen flows, not able to leave the paper. I find by the end of writing some hour later, that I have written another chapter for my book – Allowing Space to Grieve – something in this modern society that we often find difficult.

Journal Entry SSG 2020

Journal Prompts

1. What grief are you moving through and where might you be in your grief cycle?

2. How can you support yourself through this?

3. Would you benefit from creating a sacred ceremony or ritual around this to witness your loss? Perhaps a Full Moon ritual. If so, what would this look like? Who would you like to be present, if any?

CHAPTER 17:

Winter Solstice

Festival of the Return of the Light

Rebirth

Tumbling and falling just like the leaves

Peeling away the last threads

I'm scared, feeling bare

"What will I become? Who will I be?"

Then soft golden light, warm and glowing falls through my crown,

And penetrates my being

Holding me

"It's frightening, it's deep"

Then the softening comes, the yielding, allowing everything to be there

I hold this sacred moment in my heart

The golden light is my heart

I feel a gentle rocking beginning deep inside my body

Gently moving, rocking me, comforting me

She is OK now

Softening, allowing, relaxing into receiving more of me

Cracks and crevices in my pelvis and hips groan

Golden light gently begins to move, expanding to welcome these places into my bowl of being

I imagine what these may be, but it is not for my mind to name

Just Be

And then there's nothing for me to do now except accept this moment

As gentle tears drop on to my palms, I receive all of me

And I am not alone

The Universe has not abandoned me

It is all around me, cradling me

The Earth beneath me

Solid in her reverence for me

We stand together through eons of time, united in heart and womb

Holding the space for what is to come

Who I am to be as I am born again from the depths, I will surely rise again

Triumphant, renewed, rejoicing in my acceptance of all what has been and all that I am to be

Knowing I am born of the strength of my own darkness

Knowing this has shaped me perfectly into who I am

For now, I sit in trust

Just as a foetus rests in her mother's womb, cradled, safe and loved

I will be born again at the perfect time.

The Winter Solstice

Having journeyed from late Autumn and Samhain we find ourselves in late December, deep in Winter. This is the peak of Winter, when all is bare. The ground is hard with frost and snow. There is a deep quiet and stillness. The Earth is truly asleep ... or is She?

Deep within the Earth changes are taking place. The Winter Solstice falls on 21st December when we experience the shortest day and the longest night. We have arrived at the peak of darkness. At this pivotal point the Sun ceases its descent and there is a pause before it begins ever so slowly to climb the skies once more to shower its rays of light and warmth on the land.

In ancient times and still to this day, we celebrate the Winter Solstice/Yule when the Sun God returns, bringing light and renewed hope. A time for celebration as the cycles of life change once more.

I always find the Winter Solstice very magical, for there is a still point between the darkness peaking and the Sunlight returning. From darkness all is born and I can feel the magic of creation stirring in its sleep awakening to the new Sun.

Within me, I acknowledge the power of the dark phase and what it teaches me, how I have embraced and healed more of my own shadow. I am grateful for this, as it has facilitated more balance within.

As the light of the new Sun emerges, so too our inner light is reborn.

I light a candle and dedicate it with my new hopes and dreams for the coming Spring. When I finally blow out the candle, I watch the swirling smoke dance up taking with it my hopes and wishes for me and a better world.

The Solstice is a time to celebrate this magical turning point in the natural world. We are halfway through Winter, but the focus is now on renewed hope, as we call in our dreams and the promise they will bring.

Honouring and celebrating the Sun's return, brings us closer to our true cyclical nature. Being close to Nature, our lives become simpler and more harmonious, for we are flowing with the natural rhythms of the planet.

Here are some ideas for celebrating the Winter Solstice and embracing the magic and stillness of this cycle in our lives.

Celebrate the Winter Solstice!

You can create a simple ritual on your own or with family and friends. You can expand or adapt it to your own needs. As with all ceremonies and rituals the important ingredient is to be clear of your intentions.

However you wish to celebrate, take time to:

- Acknowledge the lessons of the Winter darkness so far
- Welcome the Sun's return and your own rebirth.

You'll find several ways you can celebrate the Solstice, with or without others. You can use the suggestions below and weave your own personal celebration that works for you.

Winter Solstice Celebrations:

Watch the Sunrise

Rise early to welcome the magic of the Sunrise on the Solstice. Feel the Sun's light bless you, receiving its light codes to energise and awaken your energy body. Become one with the Sun and its magnificence. Be grateful for this wonder of Nature. Send your hopes and prayers up into the ether, whilst smudging away the past with White Sage sacred herb.

Celebrating in Sacred Space

Choose a time to gather with others when it is dusk or dark, so you can enjoy the magical atmosphere and peace.

Create a central fire, paying attention to safety.

Alternatively, offer tea lights for each person, placing them on a safe surface. Create the sacred space by sitting in a circle around the candles.

Call in the energies you wish to work with. Mother Earth, Gaia and the Sun, honouring the return of the Sun God and giving thanks to the wisdom of darkness.

Invite each person to light a candle and declare their wishes to the light (either in their mind or spoken to the group).

Let the candlelight continue to burn safely for some time.

Tell stories of the old, sing and dance around the candles, celebrating the return of the Light!

Quiet Reflection – Group or Personal

If you prefer a quieter affair, you may like to create a quiet space for reflection and stillness. If you are inviting others to join you, it is easier if someone leads the ceremony.

Once the sacred space is set up, invite people to reflect on their experience of the Winter and what it has meant for them.

What have been the gifts of this phase?

What have you enjoyed?

What have you found difficult?

What have been the lessons?

You may decide to share your experiences. If so, take turns to listen to each other, gently acknowledging, witnessing each other, without questioning.

As facilitator, I like to honour each person's turn either with a Talking Stick (made from sacred wood and crystals) or by sounding my Tibetan bowl when each person finishes.

- **Family Celebration**

If you come together as a family, this is a beautiful opportunity to share your appreciation of each other and what each brings to the family unit. If speaking out loud doesn't feel so comfortable, you could write down your thoughts and feelings on strips of paper, with or without your name and add them to a central bowl. Then each person could take in turn to pull a strip and read it out loud. This way creates a safe way to share your gratitude.

Equally, if there are any grievances or difficulties you would like to make peace with, this could be a safe place to forgive each other and let go of differences and enter a new phase of peace. Set the ground rules first. This is not intended as a space to argue, but to gently share how you feel, taking responsibility for what you feel, without judgement eg 'When this happened, I felt...... I would now like to lay this to rest and make peace with you.'

Forgiveness is powerful. It serves no-one to hold onto grievances.

If you are doing this on your own, you can approach the ritual in the same way, using the space for quiet inner reflection, enjoying the stillness of the moment, appreciating all of yourself and forgiving yourself.

• Hopes and Wishes

Once you have finished reflecting and/or sharing your appreciation of each other and the Winter phase, turn your attention to welcoming the Sun's returning and what this means to you.

What hopes and wishes does your heart long for?

What kind of world do you want to live in?

Visualise this and what this would look and feel like.

As a group you can hold a few minutes' silence to visualise a peaceful, balanced and abundant Earth, in the centre of your circle.

• Prayer Ribbons

Prayer ribbons are a beautiful way to energise your prayers and intentions.

You can hang them on your Christmas tree or a tree in your garden or that you have befriended in your local park or woods. You can also write your wishes on paper or card and hang these up too. We have done this family ritual for a few years, and it is lovely to see the different coloured ribbons blowing in the breeze and to watch them through the changing seasons.

Let them be taken by the wind and rain and blanched by the sun. Each element playing its part.

• How to Make Your Prayer Ribbon

Firstly, find any piece of coloured ribbon that you would like to use that will be long enough to tie around a small branch of a tree. Tie loosely so that the tree has room to grow.

Ideally, find ribbons made of natural fibres that decompose easily. Alternatively, using a long piece of garden string, and a piece of cotton thread, tie pinecones, shells, stones with holes and feathers to the string and hang it so that they catch the breeze.

The purpose of the prayer ribbon is to imbue the ribbon with the energy of your hopes and wishes so that when you hang it on the tree, your wishes are taken by the wind and by the rain out into the world and grounded into the Earth so that they can manifest at the perfect time for you.

In the sacred space you have created, place the ribbons with the candles in the middle of your circle.

Before you begin, each person chooses a piece of coloured ribbon and holds it in their lap. When you are thinking about your hopes and wishes, hold the ribbon between your fingers and allow your heart to feel the experience now, of your wishes having been granted. Imagine your wishes are flowing into the ribbon. Be clear about your wishes as the clarity will be transmitted to the ribbon.

When you are ready, you can hang up your prayer ribbons in your chosen place.

Sacred Prayers – Setting New Intentions

'Energy Follows Thought'

We are powerful co-creators of our reality – for what we think, we become. Energy follows thought, so it is important to be mindful of the thoughts and beliefs we hold. The more we can focus on what we do want the more we can attract that to us.

When we start writing our wish list, it is worth looking underneath and seeing what that new something would bring us. Such as when we changed our car, we wanted something which was smaller and more economical, and this signified a desire to simplify our life. The dog that my daughter wanted was her need to have a loyal friend, to keep her company and to play with. Sometimes when we recognise the underlying need, we can let go of our need for it to be met in a specific way. When we ask for what we really want, we are then open to how the Universe and our Soul wishes that need to be met.

I know one lady was exploring adoption and fostering but due to financial constraints and a lack of local practical support, she wasn't considered a suitable candidate. Instead, the Universe gifted her a beautiful dog companion that is now her loyal and loving friend.

I like to focus on bringing positive qualities into my life through my inner healing. For example, "I love and accept myself unconditionally," or "I have the confidence and belief to finish this book and get it published."

Others might include, wanting more balance and peace in our life.

What would that look and feel like?

The clearer we are about what we want, the more likely we will know when we have found it.

Spend some time getting clear about what you truly want. Here are some examples to be getting on with:

Create More Fun for Yourself

What does fun look and feel like to you?

Is it a new activity that will help you express your creativity?

Does it include doing it with friends or family?

Playfulness

Bring in the energy of play by connecting with your inner magical child.

Create pauses for rest and play between chores or work tasks that bring in fun and laughter.

I remember when our children were young it was important to just forget all the chores and get down on my hands and knees and have a boisterous romp on the lounge floor. It always ended up with us having the giggles, even though I had sore knees!

Creative Expression

Make time for the things you are passionate about.

Develop your creativity eg painting, cooking, craft, making things with the children.

Consider what new beliefs you wish to hold – 'I believe in my ability to achieve......

Commit to having firm boundaries so that you have more space for quality time and your dreams to flourish. Do more things that give you pleasure. You deserve it!

Self-Nourishment

You are what you eat.

What nourishing and nutritious food can support your health and wellness?

Develop time for exercise that you enjoy eg walking in Nature, swimming, yoga and create a routine that you can commit to.

The Spirit of Christmas

Christmas Day follows quickly after the Solstice, bringing the excitement of festivities and time with family. This can feel a mixed affair, as there is so much commercialism and expectation. It is good to feel into the spirit of Christmas, of the giving and receiving of love and having quality time with family and friends. Sadly, for some it can feel a stressful and tiring experience, catering and spending a concentrated time with family that can bring irritations and old grievances to the surface. It is important to honour how you feel and give yourself space when you can, to rest and be, so you can replenish.

Journal Entry - My Walk on Christmas Day

'We had eaten our Christmas dinner and we were feeling stuffed! Amazing how much time is put into preparing the feast, only to be consumed with gusto minutes later! Christmas songs added to the merry mix. We sat there, the four of us, not able to move or speak anymore for our bellies full and our mouths now motionless, silenced by the enormity of the digestive process that had just started. A sleepy haze fell upon us, pulling us deeper into our chairs. Flames flickered from the central candle and sitting beside it I admired the simple beauty of the red berries and green and white leaves of the Pittosporum that I had gathered from our garden and placed in a slim vase a little while before. Amongst the glistening baubles and shining ribbons from the crackers, it was the fresh aliveness of the red berries that lured me into a state of grace, of wonder and I imagined myself taking a walk. The call of Mother Earth beckoned me to step outside and be with her, and so I did.

With my thick wool scarf flung around my neck and my Winter jacket, I grabbed my phone and left. As soon as I was out, I felt the presence of stillness in the air all around me. I imagined families still around the Christmas table, eating and laughing, tucked up in their warm homes, while I was out savouring a different flavour – one of peace and communion with all living things.

The sky was grey and the air felt heavy with a fine mist as if rain was about to fall. Like a soft veil of droplets, it clung in the air and around my face, and I pulled my scarf closer around me. I could hear some birds' gentle trilling and as I gazed upwards I saw two chaffinches in the roof tops of a nearby tree. I loved the trill of the birds. They reminded me of my childhood innocence when I used to love being in the garden with my favourite apple tree. It was a feeling of reassurance; they are my friends and I greeted them with a warm heart and hello.

As I approached the small woods at the end of our road, I noticed over a fence this overhanging branch full of white and pink coloured flowers – each little flower creating a large expansive bloom. I stopped and reached down to cup one bloom in my hand to see if it had a scent. To my surprise and delight, I drank deep this delicious almond sweetness. The scent filled my nostrils and went deep into my lungs, filling them with its sublime fragrance. My heart immediately responded by opening and expanding to this deliciousness. What a gift! My heart swelled and opened like a flower too responding to the invitation of this gift. I felt at one with the flower, the sweetness of all Life and the beauty of Mother Nature that had created this. It felt like I had taken a step into the heart of the Earth itself, drinking and receiving the beautiful love that she offers.

A sense of joy filled me and lightened my step as I carried on to marvel at all the other delights Mother Nature had to offer. The dark glossy, prickly leaves of the holly bush and the pine needles under my feet that created a soft carpet to walk upon.

As I entered the woods I stopped to listen. Silence! Stillness! Magic as the Earth breathed. I could hear her, feel her, as my heart quickened and skipped a beat and then settled into a gentle beat in tune with her rhythm. Feeling grateful for the privilege of this special moment that I was only sharing with Mother.

Feeling satisfied, realising the purpose of my walk fulfilled, a deep communion with the greatest Mother of all, I gave thanks and made my walk home, feeling blessed.'

Journal Entry SSG 25.12.18

We Resi io Creaie

We are now in the New Year which brings its own excitement.

For many, now that Christmas has gone, we are ready to put the past year behind us and set new goals and resolutions for the year ahead. This can spur us on initially. We feel the push to get clear our goals and plans for the New Year, leaving the past behind. We may judge ourselves for not being further ahead than we are. However, we are still in deep Winter.

This is a time to be **patient**.

Although the light is gradually returning, we need time and rest to integrate all the inner healing we experienced from Samhain to the Solstice. Because of our busy lifestyles, we may feel tired and unrested from often frantic activity leading up to the end of the calendar year.

We are over halfway through Winter, now on our journey to the regrowth of Spring. Earth is still sleeping, cold and quiet. Deep within, She is gestating.

Each one of us is unique and it is important to tune in daily to what our heart and body is calling for us and the pace She wants to lead. Just as Mother Nature gently unfurls, our body is our feminine temple and needs spaciousness to unfurl in her own precious time.

Instead of blindly leading from the head, our journey must be with our body and our need to pace ourselves, go slowly and rest in between. When we sink into the silence of our womb, we connect with the cosmic womb and the void of infinite possibilities. What is gestating deep within?

Journal Prompts

Pause, reflect, and tune in.

What questions would your Wise Woman want to ask?

What guidance can she offer you at this point in Winter?

What does she want to create?

CHAPTER 18:
Cosmic Womb – Resting in the Void

In the Beginning

Deep within

I hear the primordial sound of Mother's heartbeat

A steady heartbeat, that gently cradles and rocks me

I am held within the still centre of the cosmic rhythm

A deep knowing within the womb of cosmic creation.

A stillness born from the deep

This primordial sound of creation that births everything into Being

Nurtured, effortless, unfurling

From the never-ending infinite blackness of Nothing

Comes the first spark of Light,

The first breath of Life

The umbilical cord that connects us all to the Oneness of All

Our womb carries the key

Of Infinite possibilities

You, me, our daughters, mothers, grandmothers, and the Ancient Mother of Old

Co-creating as One

We hold the key

We are the key

To a new way, a new Earth

Never-ending cycle of death and becoming

Of dying to become still

Birthed from the Cosmic womb

When we sink into the silence of our womb, we connect with the Cosmic Womb of infinite possibilities. This is our sacred womb power. It is time to dream a new reality into being.

The Cosmic Womb

The mysteries of the Cosmic Womb that birthed us is held in our wombs – we carry the holographic blueprint of the energy of Creation, with all the mysteries of our universal existence. We have direct access to the power of the Cosmic Womb and her infinite possibilities through our sacred wombs. When we heal and honour our sacred womb, we activate her sacred purpose and open ourselves to birth profound new creations into Life, beyond just the physical – it allows women to create on the mental, emotional, psychic, and soulful planes, on both a personal and collective level. We are the midwives and co-creators of our new Earth. Through intention we create, like a droplet in an expansive ocean that ripples out through eternity.

'Through intention we create'

As we rest in the heart and Womb of Creation herself, we feel her infinite love wrap around us. Creation holds the blueprint for infinite possibility. Here, everything is happening in one time, in circular rather than linear time; there is no past or future, only the moment we are experiencing now. Within the liquid blackness, I see spirals of creation like the birthing of new stars. Our wombs remember the way home to innocence, to love, to expansiveness as we become infinite consciousness ourselves. It is time to create what we desire – to dream a bigger dream of beauty, of peace and living a life of love, joy, and abundance for all.

How Do I Connect with the Cosmic Womb?

As you become used to connecting more deeply with your womb and participate regularly in some of the suggested womb healing exercises, we awaken and remember her sacred power and potential. When she is open, you will naturally merge with the Cosmic Womb for, she exists within you already.

Meditation with the Cosmic Womb

Create a sacred space preferably in the dark or you could wear an eye mask to keep daylight out.

Take time to set up your space that is comfortable and relaxing, when you know you won't be disturbed.

Lay down with your knees bent, if this feels comfortable, with your feet planted on the ground.

Take some nice long deep breaths to settle yourself.

Give yourself permission to let go and relax fully and completely.

Begin taking the breath down into your womb, which hopefully will be a familiar place to go now.

Feel yourself enter your womb and rest deep within the darkness of your womb. Gradually feel her expanding through your breath, intending that you merge with the Cosmic Womb and Mother of Creation.

You can also imagine you are connecting with the Womb of the Earth as this is also a portal to the Cosmic Womb, for all is birthed from here.

Keep your breath soft and relaxed. Let go of trying and allow yourself to rest and drop into the darkness.

Feel yourself gradually merge into the nothingness of infinite space. Feel held and safe, nothing to do but just be in this one moment.

You may feel nothing, or you may feel the sense of the great Cosmic Mother presence all around you, holding you. The presence of Oneness where you are connected to All. Let go even more and become receptive. This is a place to deeply rest and be. There is nothing you need do just be open to receive whatever your Soul wants you to receive.

Stay here for as long as you desire to receive the feeling of expansion and oneness with creation.

When you are ready, take some deep breaths to bring yourself back into your body. Take your time to be fully grounded in your body before moving.

Note down any impressions and insights in your journal. Notice how this experience affects how you feel in your body and heart.

Dream Seeds

You may decide another time to connect with the Cosmic Womb and drop some intentions in the infinite space. Choose carefully what you wish to manifest and always for your highest good.

Alberto Villoldo, the Founder of world-renowned Four Winds Society and Light Body School is a modern-day Shaman having travelled the Amazon jungle to learn the skills and wisdom of indigenous tribes and medicine women and men that lived there. Listening to a recent webinar of his, he shared that the ancient shamans 'dream beauty for the world as a whole,' a world that feeds the hungry children, that brings peace where there are wars, and then dreaming on behalf of their village before they dream for themselves. 'Abundance is not how much is in your bank account but how much you give and the abundance one holds in your heart.'

Consider your intentions for the world you want to live in, for your community and for your family. Then consider your own dreams and how they contribute to the whole. I invite you to write these in your journal before meditating and then your consciousness is already carrying the energetic imprint of your dream seeds.

Connecting to Other Dimensions

We can access other dimensions through our womb and the Cosmic Womb. I recall holding space for a woman, guiding her to connect with her womb and the Cosmic Womb. She travelled into infinite space and connected with her star lineage, connected with the Star Andromeda where she felt completely at home. She experienced a most beautiful reunion with a fellow star being who she spent some time being in deep communion. She received an activation and a remembering of her connection with this beautiful star constellation, that she once called home. She received keys and activations to awaken what was dormant within her that would help her assist others in her sacred work with women.

Consciously working with our dreams in this way is what is most fascinating. Through deep meditation and journeying into the infinite quantum field of the Cosmic Womb, where everything is possible, we begin to co-create a new reality for the world and ourselves. We can do this at any time of the year, but Winter is a potent time to sow new dream seeds that will eventually flower in the growth months of the year.

We can choose to journey through our sacred wombs to the Cosmic Womb of creation in our meditation during the day, or we can choose to consciously dream at night.

Conscious Dreaming

Tap into the stillness, into the void of dreamtime, to create a new reality into being. Our dream seeds gestate deep inside.

Dreaming

We all dream, whether we consciously remember or not. Our dreams are a mirror of our earthly reality helping us to process information and daily occurrences to free up the mind. Dreams also offer a way to connect more deeply with the wisdom of our Soul and our connection with the Oneness of the Universe.

According to the National Sleep Foundation, we typically dream about four to six times per night, although most of the time we don't remember our dreams. Most of our dreams occur during our REM sleep (rapid eye movement), which helps our brain consolidate and process new information.

There are different types of dreams, including our normal nightly dreams, nightmares, night terrors and then there is lucid dreaming and conscious dreaming.

Most people's nightly dreams are expressed visually through colour although some are in black and white. You may experience strong emotions and feelings during your dreams. The less stressed we are, the more pleasant our dreams are likely to be. Dreams can be very strange; the unconscious mind finds unusual ways to process the day, that may involve people you have connected with recently and incidents with family and friends. What we watch on TV or read, may also trigger a dream response using aspects of ourselves played out by different characters.

Depending on your stress levels, you may have dreams that display a level of anxiety such as being chased, feeling you've missed a deadline or missed a bus, feeling lost and fearful. These are all useful signs of what we are experiencing in our daily life, or may be surfacing from childhood or previous lives for healing and resolution. Take note of these as you can use the opportunity to do some inner healing or seek support from a professional, particularly if they are reccurring dreams. This is one way our higher mind is trying to gain our attention.

Sometimes we experience nightmares when we wake suddenly from a frightening dream. Watching or reading something scary before bedtime can trigger these and those that suffer from post-traumatic stress disorder (PTSD) can experience repeated nightmares and may need to seek professional help to move forward. Night terrors are usually more related to young children going through a phase. Often this can occur if the child is finding it difficult to express their fears in the day. Encouraging them to express their fears and hopes through drawing with crayons or role play can be a helpful and a safe way for them to access and express these unconscious fears.

Lucid Dreaming – Conscious Dreaming

In the infinite space of the void, known as the quantum field, all is connected in Oneness. According to Dr. Joe Dispenza, the quantum field "is an invisible field of energy and information—or you could say a field of intelligence or consciousness—that exists beyond space and time."

Lucid dreaming is dreaming with awareness, and with practice, we can help control our dreams and influence the outcome we desire. Lucid dreaming is something our ancestors have done for thousands of years and still practiced by indigenous culture around the world today. Lucid dreaming is a shamanic skill, a method of heightened awareness in the dream, allowing healers and medicine men and women insight, wisdom, and information to influence a new reality. They travel with their soul light body, beyond time and space to connect with the infinite void, to receive signs, messages and insights, healing, and medicine to assist the Earth and her kingdoms and those in their community. Many ancient cultures, including the Mayans have prophesied about significant changes on Earth. It is believed they travel beyond time and space to the origins of creation and to other timelines, giving them insights to the different possibilities of what is unfolding on Earth.

Some people can foresee catastrophic events in their dreams. This could be seeing a friend's accident or on a much larger scale, earthquakes and tsunami, or other significant events impacting the world.

When I went on an online Active Dreaming course with Monica Kenton, an Active Dreaming Teacher who studied with Robert Moss, I learnt some of the benefits of working with our dreams consciously. We can use these skills to deepen our connection with our Soul, open to what else is possible for us to dream, with play and curiosity.

What do you want to consciously dream?

Dream – Setting Clear Intentions

Having a clear intention before going to sleep acts as a focus for your energy. It is a way to communicate with your soul. Ask yourself these questions and note them down in a Dream Journal before going to bed:

What do I want my dream to tell/show me?

What experience is going to be beneficial for my Soul's path?

What issue/problem am I experiencing, that I need help with?

We can also prepare ourselves to remember our dreams by setting a clear intention before we go to sleep.

You may like to use this prayer, or something similar, that sets safe boundaries for your dream journey into other realms.

Dream Prayer

"I ask my spiritual team to open the gates and portals to my dreams that serve to nourish my mind, body, and soul. All gateways that may cause harm or damage to me or loved ones remain closed. And so it is."

Dream Journal

Memories of dreams usually fade very quickly after we awake, so having a Dream Journal and pen next to your bed is a great way to catch some of the immediate impressions, signs, and feelings you experience. Many of us don't recall our dreams but working with intention helps us to wake up to important messages. Some dream recall is vivid, and these are easier to note down upon waking. Other times we only get dream fragments, but I have found these are equally helpful when noted, as when pieced together, offer meaning and wisdom conveyed in the dream. They may express what is currently being healed in your dream.

Dream Interpretations

In one of my dreams, I asked to experience the Void and all its potential.

What I did not expect was to experience both the Light and Dark but because my intention was broad, anything was possible. My dream showed me the infinite potential of what is possible to create and that we can choose to create from both dark and light.

In this dream, I experienced the two extremes; the dark in this case that felt like an aspect of the Collective Consciousness where the patriarchy of control and greed was playing out. It was dark and murky, and I saw people asleep, being controlled. There was a lot of fear in this dream that I could feel. I quickly left that dream only to find I was in another dream. The second dream was full of bright light, and I saw seeds of new growth in the shape of small light pods, representing the cocoon of gestating new life.

These dreams showed me the power of choice that we have. What do we choose to create? Do we choose to stay asleep, allowing others to control and suppress our free will, or do we choose to create beauty, peace, love and a world filled with light?

What will you choose to create?

Before you go on a dream journey, it is good to ask your spiritual team to be with you on your dream journey while you sleep. My luminous light body is my travelling bubble. I have also been shown that I am placed in a Light Pod that I can travel in. As part of your prayer for Dreaming, ask your spiritual team and guides or a power animal to travel with you, so that you receive dreams that are a positive contribution to your own healing and spiritual growth.

This is particularly helpful if you are doing a lot of healing work for the collective in your sleep. Many of us lightworkers do this without consciously knowing where we travel. We can wake up feeling tired as if we have done a night's work! In the morning, it is helpful to ask for any portals that have been opened, to be closed so you are grounded in this earthly reality.

If you find in your dream you don't remember the whole of it, note down the pieces you do recall. You can go back into the dream journey and ask further questions. Allow your higher self and spirit to guide you to create a different outcome that helps you overcome some reccurring anxiety. Call upon your spirit guides and power animals to assist you. They can be great at offering you wisdom and the gift of their strength and courage to overcome problems.

Meaning of Dreams

I experienced a further vivid dream that I recalled in detail on waking.

I was the observer in the dream, watching what unfolded.

I felt I was in the underworld. Although dark, there was a soft light emanating everywhere. There were otherworldly beings, together with what I sensed was a man. He was suspended in the air with his hands tied behind his back. As I watched, this web-like material was covering his eyes until he could no longer see. I felt there was a lot of fear in the dream, although being the observer, I didn't experience it fully. It certainly felt weird though. Then in Dreamtime, the web-like material disappeared to reveal three eyes in a row across his forehead. He had blood red and gold spirals pouring out of his mouth.

At this point in the dream, I woke suddenly.

Giving your dream a name is a great way to bring home the message of your unconscious mind. What is the key message being conveyed? What is the dominant feeling during it?

In this dream I gave the title 'The Awakening' – not the obvious choice looking from the outside but when I asked myself the question, 'What title shall I give this dream,' this is what I received.

First, I noted all the key elements of the dream and how I felt.

Then I gave it the title.

I then went through to explore what the different aspects meant.

The covering of the eyes with the web-like material – on reflection felt like the creative web of a spider or cocoon that then revealed something new, a transformation, hence the 'awakening.'

I had been working with my masculine energy, healing old wounds and grief so he/I could step more fully into his power. The eyes represented the third eye and revealing greater vision and psychic ability.

His tied hands seemed to represent how he had been controlled and suppressed, perhaps in the past, and his fear of being out of control.

I spoke with my soulful healer as I had been working with her over a few months to see what additional reflections she might have. She confirmed that the unconscious was conveying a message of the key work we had done together and the transformation I had experienced, and she had witnessed. The red and gold energy flowing from his mouth connected with my root and kundalini energy that I was now fully expressing in my life.

Shamanic Journeying

The Shamans would take a shamanic journey to connect with spirit guides and power animals to help with healing. They would prepare themselves by smudging their aura, creating sacred space, and offering a Sacred Prayer up to Spirit. They would call in their guides, their star brothers and sisters or spirit animals to ask for help for an individual in their community or to help with crops or any other issue of suffering they felt the world was facing. Sometimes they would journey to receive prophecy of what is to come, so they could prepare.

In my Shamanic drum circles, I guide women on a similar Shamanic journey with the sound of the drum beat as their guide. We hold a prayer lightly in our hearts and minds that acts as the arrow of focus for our shamanic journey. Each woman experiences their own unique journey, whether they need to experience healing, receive wisdom and insights, or a new perspective. Some experience visualisations of colour and animal spirits who have come to offer their gifts of healing. Others deeply rest in the energy of the journey, trusting that their mind, body, and Soul receives what they need.

You can create your own Dream Journey by playing music with a repetitive drumbeat.

You can go to my website for a Shamanic Drum Journey audio recording, a link can be found at the back of the book under Resources.

Queen of Winter – The Goddess Cailleach

The Goddess Cailleach is known as the Queen of Winter and sometimes The Veiled One. Appearing as an old, veiled woman, she reigns over the winds and Winter. She is both destroyer and creator but, in this context, I see her as the great Mother Creator. She stands at the gateway into the Cosmic Womb and Dreamtime where we co-create with the Universe allowing what wants to come forward for birthing.

Cailleach is the Grandmother Weaver of Earth and the Cosmos, helping us to connect with our Star Ancestors for nourishment from the Galactic Heart. In my journeys with her, I see her like the Snow Queen, reflecting the Light of the stars and Cosmos in her long hair so that we may be open and inspired by our multi-dimensional nature. She helps the gestation of our dream seeds so that come Imbolc, in the early weeks of Spring, the Goddess Brigid is ready to breathe life into them with her Sacred Flame.

The Milky Way is the Cosmic Mother's nourishing milk that feeds the Soul. When we allow more space for rest, our bodies regenerate and our soul grows and expands. We take our place within the Net of Light that is the web around our planet. Gradually our purpose becomes clearer.

All that we are to experience will come at the perfect time.

The way to connect to Dreamtime is to welcome stillness into our day.

The Magic of Stillness

One of the blessings of Winter is a time to rest and become still. She offers a beautiful time for us to press pause, to heal and reset. Once we do this, we can begin to see what we no longer need, what we can let go of and what is ready to be dreamed into being. It is when we create moments of stillness within, that we open a new blank page in our Book of Life which allows us to receive new ideas from the Universe.

Within each person there's a quiet place where we can access a deep stillness. When we consciously choose to push away outside distractions and noise, we can more easily flow with Winter's rhythm of deep resting, supported by her energy.

In Winter, I have a natural tendency to withdraw within. Perhaps with years of practice of being in tune with the Earth's cycles it has become easier to listen to what my body is calling me for.

Having a morning practice where we choose to meet ourselves, is a beautiful way to deepen our relationship with Self and start the day as we mean to go on. Rather than first thing checking your email and messages, create space to greet yourself, to tune in, to say good morning to your heart and body like you would a good friend. It's a wonderful way to stay in connection with yourself and the Earth. Connecting to stillness within allows calmness to flow into your day.

"I allow my heart to rest in stillness so that peace flows through my day."

Sometimes, we go through phases of craving connection and love with others or our partner, when really there's a deep need within for connection with self. When we fulfil the need within ourselves, we no longer need that "fix" from outside. It comes from a different place of conscious awareness rather than a need that wants to be fulfilled. Such as when we might reach for chocolate, biscuits or want to veg out in front of the TV. These are not bad in moderation. It is worth asking ourselves the question:

"What need am I wanting fulfilled here?"

"What will x give me that I am seeking?"

"What would happen if I didn't connect with or have x? How would I feel?

In this way, we begin to understand the underlying patterns and habitual urgings that are driving our choices and behaviours and begin to change them.

Quality of Stillness

When we dive in to connect with ourselves, initially we may find it difficult to connect with peace and stillness. Like when you initially connect with your womb, you may find you experience emotions, feelings and sensations that are far from peaceful. Stick with her though. Be in presence with all that you are, for the stillness comes from a place of **allowing** everything to be there and with **acceptance**.

When I am holding space for other women, I always encourage a space of openness and trust where everything is welcome whether it is sadness, hurt, grief, anger, frustration and equally joy, love, laughter and pleasure – nothing is too much. For when we deny our true feelings, we betray our own sense of self. We reject ourselves.

> *"It is time to honour the whole of me, knowing I am beauty inside and out."*

Being still allows us to come back home to our heart, to feel what we feel, what is real and raw, to be with what arises without judgement but with compassion. From this place of acceptance, whatever we are experiencing can soften and relax, helping us to move beyond and touch the true essence of our Soul where stillness and peace always resides.

Stillness is where we meet the Universe, where we let go of thoughts and enter the eternal field of Oneness where we get to co-create in the field of infinite possibilities.

We go inside to reach out and connect. Within our heart/womb space there is infinite space and opportunity always for connection.

What is Stillness?

What is stillness to you?

It's a refreshing sleep.

It's when our consciousness merges with Universal consciousness.

It's a still lake; just like throwing a round pebble into the waters creates a ripple effect, so too do our thoughts, prayers and intentions that ripple out into the Universal collective field.

> *Drop an intention or prayer without attachment or expectation*
> *and allow the magical synchronicities in your life to unfold.*

Stillness is the void.

It's the quiet mind.

It's the dark womb of Mother.

It's here we touch the creative potential of our Divine Feminine for we are born from the Dark Mother and the Cosmic Womb.

How Do We Connect with Stillness?

What is stillness?

Stillness is when there is a moment of peace or tranquillity, often when the mind is quiet, and there is no noise to distract you from being with yourself. A connection that is always available to us deep in our hearts. When we rest and listen.

We can connect more easily with the quality of stillness when we are in Nature, listening to the sounds of the comings and goings of birds and animals and the sounds of gently swaying trees in the breeze. For me, it creates a gentle soothing sound that is the thrum and hum of creation all around me. We are part of creation's whole, and so at some deep level we feel held in stillness. Between the sounds of the thrum of Nature, the spaces in between the fabric and web of creation, I invite you to slip through a portal beyond time and space, to infinite oneness and peace.

What does stillness mean to you?

How do you create space for stillness to blossom in your day?

Are there places and spaces that you are drawn to, that help you connect with the stillness and peace inside?

To discover what creates stillness for you, you may like to do some journalling on this to discover what helps you.

I did a little post on Facebook to find out what 'stillness' meant to people and discovered quite a few things.

Some people create space at the end of their day with a cup of tea or favourite drink to sit and contemplate, to empty their mind and let their thoughts drift, perhaps listening to music to help them feel calm and at peace.

Others find stillness, in different circumstances – one woman found several ways she connected with stillness.... By being in her beautiful home, out browsing at a local quirky market, doing things that made her happy, even daydreaming out of the window while sitting on the loo. I loved this one, as there is a sense of letting go and allowing the mind to drift along with the clouds.

Some people use mindfulness techniques to focus the mind and the breath. This was particularly useful for one woman who when younger suffered from ADHD (Attention deficit hyperactivity disorder). She found it very difficult to sit still for very long and although challenging at first, she learnt to practice Mindfulness, to slow down her breath and to focus on the simple things and objects to discover beauty is simply everywhere. This helped her take in the pleasure of her environment.

For example, she started appreciating flowers which was a significant change for her, as in the past, she never paid any attention to her husband who regularly bought her flowers. Since he passed away, she is appreciating flowers so much more which naturally holds the memory of his love and his previous acts of kindness.

Another lady having suffered a physical injury, found it challenging to sit still with herself. Over time, she has learnt to turn this challenge into an act of self-kindness. By paying attention to the whole of herself, consciously gathering and connecting with all parts of herself through awareness and the breath, she has gifted herself self-compassion and most importantly **self-acceptance** by being in the moment. Through nurturing herself, understanding her beliefs and reactions, she has begun to let go of what she's been holding onto for other people. And her body is learning to relax and be still as she safely allows herself to let go of past trauma.

When we allow, listen, and accept, we find peace.

Simple Breath Exercise

Deep breath in through your nose

Out through your mouth

Let go

Pause

Deep breath in

Let go

Pause

Repeat a few times. Give yourself permission to sigh out.

Can you begin to connect with a feeling of stillness?

What Other Ways are There to Connect with Stillness?

May be there are places in Nature that evoke feelings of stillness and tranquillity for you. Being by the sea, listening to the waves ebb and flow, is very calming for me, or any gentle running water, such as a river or stream is important for my flow. Perhaps a still lake offers a space for calm reflection.

Visiting ancient stone circles, that carry a powerful silence, is another great way to connect with peace. Walking in forests, visiting a beautiful garden or even creating your own sacred space that we discussed at the end of Part One in Creating Your Own Sacred Space is a wonderful way to reconnect with yourself and find inner stillness.

Stillness isn't necessarily about being in solitude, although sometimes you may seek your own company so you can focus on your own truth and what is arising for you.

> *Stillness is a state of being, a still pond deep in the well of our*
> *sacred heart.*

Here we connect with the silence of Oneness.

Often, we know what is good for us, or what helps us find stillness and peace, but do not create enough space in our day to do that? Does that happen for you?

We have good intentions, and then work or other people's needs distract us. When we eventually press pause and seek time with ourselves, it leads us to a greater path of ease, as I found when I was feeling restless. I chose to sit with myself instead. This is what I discovered...

Journal Eniry - 'Siillness'

*In stillness there is so much to **receive**.*

My mind has kept me busy dealing with different tasks, pulling me this way and that and I realise I don't feel settled. I feel restless, needing some way to satisfy this niggle inside.

I pause and decide to sit instead.

Dropping into the stillness of my heart, I immediately feel peace. The mind quietens and I tune into the rhythm of my breathing and the pulse of my heartbeat. I sit and listen and gradually my mind quietens, ceasing to chatter. I feel the sensations and tensions of my body. I watch and breathe, noticing as I pay attention. As the tension moves around my body, I begin to relax.

There is a sense of release as I listen to my body, as if she is saying, "At last, you've stopped, you're listening to me!"

In the quietness of my inner space, I feel the softening of my body as she relaxes even more.

I value the stillness, this quiet space for me as it allows my body to settle, for the wisdom of my heart to come forward and she says,

"In the stillness is where you hear my soul whispers, the subtle and strong sensations of my inner knowing and higher wisdom. I open to the light pouring in from my higher self and the nourishment rising up from the Earth. I feel met and held – as above so below – in the centre of my heart.

I suddenly feel calm, my once racing heartbeat, slowly becoming in tune with the Earth's heartbeat, resting in a slow rhythmic beat.

I drop a question into my heart, taking the opportunity of the wisdom that wants to speak from the stillness,

"What is my potential? What is my future?"

Again, like many times before, I see myself smiling, happy, laughing as I come on to stage to speak and share with the many hearts in front of me. Sharing the light and wisdom of the heart from a place of solid strength, and I sense I'm supported by the tall trunk of a tree.

I see me with large groups, drumming, singing and swaying with movement, creating ceremony in gratitude. I am happy and strong.

I ask again,

"How do I get to be in this place and state of being?" I feel I'm questioning, how is this possible!

I see hands reaching out beside me as I walk my path, many hands that are there to offer their support, to steady me, to encourage and inspire me, to motivate me.

I breathe this all in, feeling the possibilities vibrate through my body and into my cells.

And,

"What do I need now?" "What is my next step?"

Listen

Trust

Walk my path in gratitude.

As I gradually come out of my resting, I realise my mind is clearer. I feel focussed, still and clear and I know what I need to do next.

I settle with my notebook to write, to capture these words and moments of creative impulses that have come to me in stillness.

Journal Entry SSG 2021

Reflections:

Stillness can be underrated when there is no tangible result to savour, observe, share or celebrate. Stillness is a quality. It connects us to our deepest essence, our truest sense of who and what we are in any given moment. It allows us to pause, to reset and begin afresh.

It can give us a sense of acceptance, of calmness that comes from the stillness. It allows us to gather the scattered pieces of our energy, to reclaim our power and light, to become the strong pillar of light, the beam of light that we are already.

Winter offers us the space to slow down, to rest more and to reconnect with the essence of stillness that always resides within us.

Stillness Practice

Create a calm and inviting space in your home where you can unwind, away from distractions. Take some time to reorganise and reprioritise your needs and space in the house for you.

Create a sacred space (See Chapter 9: *Creating your Sacred Space*) that invites you into connection with Mother Earth and Spirit.

Having a small table or floor area with a cloth, with crystals and candle and Winter foliage can create peace.

Listen to calming music or if you have a drum, you may wish to beat your drum rhythmically. Sound healing with crystal and Tibetan bowls is also a great way to quieten the mind and relax.

Candle gazing can be a beautiful way to enter stillness. Choose a candle so it is a comfortable distance in front of you that doesn't strain your eyes or neck. Begin to gaze at the centre of the flame and then the whole flame, allowing a soft gaze, observing its gentle flicker and dance or stillness. Gradually allow your eyes to soften even more so you allow your peripheral vision to take over, so you are not focussing on the flame but the flame within the room. Do this for a few minutes, then come back to focussing on the central flame.

Breathing in its warmth, light and magic into your heart.

Gently relax and bring yourself back.

Notice how you feel.

Walking in the stillness of Winter

Walk in Nature, woods, and forests to feel the stillness and softness of Nature in her Winter bareness. Feel grounded and at peace.

Observe her natural beauty as she sleeps. Marvel at a fallen tree trunk. Notice how in death she provides a home for hundreds of insects.

Look up at the trees in their bare limbs and marvel at their silent wisdom. Stand with your spine to a tree trunk and feel your roots follow the tree's roots down into the deep Earth.

Winter's Vision Quest

Just like the shamans and many indigenous cultures still do today, we can go on a Vision Quest. Traditionally, they would take themselves into Nature, a sacred space or climb up a mountain to be in quiet sanctuary for a few days or even for weeks, to commune with Great Spirit, their Creator. They would fast, perhaps just take the bare essentials, surviving from the land in order to be in communion with their Great Mother.

We don't have to climb mountains, to create our own Vision Quest. We can create our own version of a Vision Quest to withdraw from the external noise of modern-day trappings and make us receptive to hearing and feeling Great Spirit (Source or Universe, God, Goddess, however you like to refer to the greater life force in your life) in our hearts.

Creating Your Own Vision Quest

Take a short break away somewhere in the country or by the sea so you can immerse yourself in Mother Nature and allow yourself to recharge mentally, emotionally, and spiritually.

Explore a **Silent Retreat** where people come to rest in meditation and other practices whilst spending their time silent.

Organise a **Spa Day** on your own or with a close friend where you can honour peace.

Carve out time for you. If you are not able to be away from home, carve out a day or half day with no phones or electronic devices and create your own sacred space specially for your Vision Quest.

Take a **Medicine Walk in Nature**, holding an intention in your heart – for more clarity or to be receptive to how spirit wants to move and flow through you.

- Watch for signs of animals and birds and their calls, that speak to you of the magic of Winter and what you are co-creating.
- Pick up gifts left by the animal and bird kingdom – a feather, a stone, a leaf, a Winter flower, a tree – and spend time contemplating their significance for you at this time.

Journal – spending time reflecting on your life and writing possible ideas.

Express your creativity – allowing whatever wants to be expressed through you in words, song, movement, paint, or sketching. What does your Soul want to dream?

Make yourself a Winter Goddess – perhaps explore felt, needlework, or clay that you can mould into a female womb shape for sheer fun. This can be really fulfilling.

Make from Winter wood – look at suggestions under Chapter 5 on Sacred Trees in Part One for ideas on making Talking Sticks and Wands.

Pleasure – self massage, bath rituals with candlelight, song that you can bathe and drift off in peace.

Open and be receptive – let go of expectations. Allow the magic to find **you inside your**self.

Rest in stillness – resting, napping, dreaming, and daydreaming.

Journal Prompts

Use these two statements to dive into what it means to be still:

'I AM still when....'

'I touch the quality of stillness when....'

What does stillness mean to you?

Would you like more moments of stillness in your life?

Remember a time when you received your best ideas, what were you doing or being?

Where were you? What were you feeling?

Are you ready to create more moments of stillness?

Identify where you may be keeping yourself busy to avoid connecting deeper with yourself?

What one step can you take to begin to overcome this?

Make a commitment to yourself.

How much time will you dedicate per day, per week?

10 minutes, 20 or 30 minutes, or a luxurious day to yourself.

CHAPTER 19:
Winter Reflections

Winter Rituals

Let Go and Nourish Your Inner Light.

We are recognising the importance of going within to nourish and nurture during Winter's rest. When it is dark, it can feel difficult to feel motivated by the lack of light.

Do you feel that too?

Here, I share my own experience of feeling the intensity of the darkness and how I came to go within to nourish.

Journal Entry - It's Dark Outside!

The Earth and Mother Nature are becoming bare, as we move into deep darkness. The grey skies and clouds full of rain pull me down and inwards. There is little light outside but when I turn my attention inside, I see and feel something different. A warm glow of a flame, a heart flame. When I breathe into this flame it grows and flickers. This is the heart flame of love and as I pay attention within, the flame is fuelled by my breath. She brings a feeling of warmth and expansion in my heart. I feel soft. The warmth now spreads down into my stomach and belly, filling up my lower pelvic bowl. As I nourish myself in this simple act of kindness to myself, I feel warm, openhearted.

I recognise this is also the flame of alchemy – I bring the parts of myself rejected, abandoned and "not enough" into my heart. I welcome these separate parts of myself home to my heart and feel a new connection beginning. I welcome home the children of my Soul into the deep chambers of my heart, to feel whole again.

Journal Entry SSG 2019

Winter is a time to nurture our inner landscape, to prune away dead wood, and create a new space where our internal light can grow bright, true and strong.

Welcome into your heart those parts that feel separate and notice the peace and acceptance that comes by welcoming wholeness, knowing you are already whole.

Guided Meditation

Fanning the Eternal Heart Flame Ritual

Light a candle and place it in front of you where you can see it.

Sit comfortably or lie.

Focus on your breathing, taking two deep breaths. Letting out a sigh of relaxation. Now focus on your breath softening, rising, and falling gently.

Focus on the candle – it's brilliance, its gentle softness. Where do you focus your attention? – in the centre of the flame, the flickering, or the edges? Just notice what you become aware of.

Allow your gaze to soften,

Then close your eyes taking the flame inside.

Become aware of your heart.

Place your hands on your heart.

Breathe and relax the chest and heart, allowing it to also soften.

Imagine the flame softly glowing in the centre of your heart.

Feel the flame igniting your own inner heart flame – maybe a small spark is becoming brighter, as you focus your attention and your gentle breath there.

Feel how your heart flame grows brighter and stronger.

Become aware of the colour of your heart flame – is it changing? How does it feel?

Imagine the three-fold flame in your heart – blue, soft pink and gold – the merging of the Divine Feminine and Divine Masculine – bringing together into unity and birthing the third, the Divine Child.

Enjoy this sensation in your heart, as it expands to embrace your Three-fold heart flame.

When you are ready, bring yourself back, be aware of how you now feel.

Make sure you feel back in your body and your feet are connected to the floor and rooted deep into Mother Earth.

Winter Reflections

In our Winter journey, we have connected with our ancestors at Samhain and begun to let go of all that no longer serves. It has been a time of healing, letting go of our fears and embracing the parts of us we dislike or deny. With love and forgiveness, we bring the separate parts of ourselves home to our hearts, so we feel whole and at peace.

We have connected with the Light of the Winter Solstice and tapped into the magic of this transition, bringing renewed hope, ready for the forthcoming Spring. But we recognise we need to pace ourselves, to go gently, to listen inwards to what our heart and body needs. We learn to resist the push of society and honour our own inner rhythm. We turn increasingly to Mother Earth for her guidance and wisdom. We are learning to hear and feel her pulse that naturally guides us to value our feminine power and inner wisdom.

As we reflect now, we give thanks for the lessons of past challenges that have helped us become stronger and wiser and shaped the woman we are today.

We recognise the power of resting and Dreamtime, allowing space for new hopes and dreams to rise from our womb and heart's fertile space.

Key Gifts of Winter

Let go of resistance and welcome the regenerative power of Winter's darkness. Allow her to become your friend.

Welcome and accept this dark phase, enjoy the rest and nourishment this cycle brings.

Journey deep to meet those places within that need healing and completing in your life. Forgive and let go.

Allow yourself to receive.

Give yourself permission to slow down, give space and time for your inner healing.

To feel nourished and held by the Great Mother herself.

Follow in Nature's footsteps.

Rest and nourish yourself on all levels.

Enjoy the stillness within.

Winter Journal Prompts

What is your current perception of the Winter season? How does it affect your mood?

How can you benefit personally from this Winter phase?

What can you do differently this Winter to nourish your inner wellbeing?

Having read and absorbed this Winter section, what were the key things that jumped out at you that you would like to pay attention to?

What changes are you committed to taking?

CHAPTER 20:
The Birthing Process

The cosmic dancer sow's seeds of new light and from this place deep in the womb of our being she gestates a new creation.

We are the cosmic dancer co-creating with the Universe.

Each Moon cycle, we feel the power of our Inner Winter phase, receiving the flows of Cosmic inspiration, some of which become the seeds for our new creations.

As multi-dimensional beings of Light we are co-creating a new way of being, a more evolved Soul that serves to radiate Light and Love in the world.

Earth's Winter offers the same spaciousness to dive in and reap the rewards of stillness, of deep nourishment and renewal. From this deep place within our Cauldron of Plenty we are gestating the most treasured gifts that we will eventually give birth to in the dawn of a new Spring.

We perceive Winter as a dark, barren place yet this is furthest from the truth. Deep down amongst the roots there is a powerful gestation and presence, as creation is creating within the fertile belly of the Earth.

*Rumi quote: "And don't think the garden loses its ecstasy in
Winter. It's quiet, but the roots are down there, riotous."*

The same applies to our female womb. Deep within, our dream seeds are gestating. We require to listen, to rest and be, to resist the need to push through. Seeing others further ahead than my own path used to trigger my lack of self-worth and this would pull me out of alignment with my Soul's path. And I received a visualisation of walking in a field of light. I felt the presence of other Souls in this field of light and yet I saw a very clear path ahead of me that I was only walking. This gave me a clear nudge and alignment that my path is unique and to stop being distracted by others. I see many women feeling the same, comparing themselves and feeling like they are left behind. We are all where we need to be. Even if we know we want things to change, we know that in this moment, we are in the perfect place and that everything is falling into place at the right time.

'In this moment, I am in the perfect place, and I know that everything is falling into place at the right time.'

We are each unique, with our own timing of gestating, sprouting, flowering and blossoming. Tuning in, listening, and following our inner yearnings as the way to nurture and nourish our creations are the keys to an effortless birth.

Flowing with the Cycle of Creation

Seed – Gestating – Sprouting – Growth – Flowering – Blossoming – Decay – Death – Renewal

In the section on Conscious Dreaming in *Chapter 18: Cosmic Womb*, we talk to the Universe, drop questions and plant seeds of new ideas in our fertile womb, and we can create ritual around this too. Just as Winter is the foundation for growth in the Spring, we must trust that we will have a successful birth at the perfect time.

We have seen during the Winter phase, the importance of surrendering to our stillness, keeping the patience as we spend time nurturing our dreams and desires.

It is important to share that we may have Winter phases in our lives, such as a major change like the Menopause. This is our time of Winter to go within to face our fears of death and decay and reclaim our Wise Wild Woman and Elder of our community.

We go through continual cycles of death and rebirth, for this is our true cyclical nature. When we know we are leading up to rebirth, our ego's fear and resistance can rise, causing us to doubt and falter. Know this can be a natural reflection of our own physical birth when we incarnated into this life.

Keep the trust and faith in your heart's calling and your deep inner knowing.

'Take the leap anyway and let the Universe catch you.'

CHAPTER 21:
Stirring in the Earth
Imbolc

Towards the end of Winter, which may vary depending on where you are in the world, we feel the undeniable signs of the Earth stirring from her Winter sleep.

Pin pricks of Winter's witch hazel with her intensely bright yellow stems glimmer in Winter's soft light. Towards the end of January here in the UK, we become witness to the first signs of pure white snowdrops. Remarkably, they push through the dark cold earth and begin to appear in woodland and parks spreading their light and hope.

I have always found the innocence and purity of the snowdrop a most beautiful sign of renewal and hope. A positive sign that ever so slowly the darkness of Winter is coming to its natural end. Hope that the dream seeds we sowed deep in Winter's fertile womb are beginning to emerge from the belly of our Mother, responding to the increasing warmth and light that lengthen our days.

Hope and the promise of all that is to come is here. In fact, it never left us. Hope journeyed with us throughout Winter in the flame of our hearts and bellies. We have been nourished and nurtured by Winter's deep rest, allowing all that was ready to go to fall away.

The Winter's frost and cold created space for us to slow down and look within, to be still and reflect. Do you feel you have managed to do this?

There is great power in being and resting.

All that we dreamed and continue to dream will emerge and unfurl with the grace of Mother's love and magic.

Imbolc signals the celebration of this turning of the Wheel. Our ancestors celebrated Imbolc meaning 'the quickening in the belly.' This new dawn of emerging Light was honoured with the Sacred Flame of the Goddess Brigid who ignites the flame of inspiration in our hearts. Journey with her now as we cross a new threshold into the promise of new beginnings.

A Sacred Prayer to Goddess Brigid

Celebrating the Light

Dear Brigid

Guardian of the Sacred Flame of Hearth and Home

May you honour this time of Rebirth

Sweep away the cloak of Winter

Let the nourishment of Winter's rest carry me.

May the joy of pure innocence of my heart guide me forward

To the promise of new lands of great beauty.

With a heart full of glee

Let the magic of my dreams be ignited

May they take form and shape with Mother's grace.

May your sacred Flame, dear Brigid

Ignite and inspire my seeds to sprout, grow and flourish

May your sacred eternal waters flow unhindered to give birth to new Life.

I give thanks for all I have received in the darkness

For now, I open my heart wide to receive

The promise and beauty of my dream seeds

That are gestating from deep within, ready to flower and blossom.

May the Light of your pure essence Bless Me.

Mother Nature is my ally.
I give thanks and praise to her
Wherever I go.

My Book Writing Journey

As I reflect now on my book writing journey, I can see how everything is perfectly aligned. It's been my Soul's journey that has taken me to my edges, allowing life to move through me, so I can write and share my life experiences and wisdom I have gained. I would not have been ready before.

My book writing journey first began back in 2010, a time when my husband and I were visiting Poole, Dorset exploring the possibility to relocate here from Surrey. At the time, we were staying in a hotel close to Poole Harbour. After having an afternoon nap, I woke with words filling my mind. They came quick and fast like flowing water, and I rushed to find a scrap of paper to pour these words onto. I remember feeling amazed at the magic they contained at the time, of childlike wonder that filled me with excitement. I recognised the power of water; the sea is and continues to be providing me inspiration for my book and my creative ideas. Back home in Surrey, my book continued to take shape, feeling the call of Mother Earth strong at the time. I recall friends and clients encouraging me too, saying this or that would be great to put in my book. We eventually took the plunge to relocate in 2012 and we have never looked back.

Before we moved, I approached an editor of a magazine who also published books to see if she would be interested. After a couple of emails, I received no response. I recall feeling my lack of confidence in my writing and fear of rejection came up. With our move looming ahead, I packed up my book where she stayed for a few years. Relocating, I needed time to establish my roots and settle our young children in their new schools. I focussed on developing my healing practice and business down here in Poole and set up a 'Creative Women in Business' networking group. This served to support me in feeling at home here and making new connections and helped the women to come together. There felt a strong calling for women to be together, to create and support each other and I loved facilitating and holding a transformative space for them to feel accepted.

Our creative ideas can lie dormant for a few years, while we flow with life. You will have your own creative ideas and big dreams too and you may wonder why they never see the light of day. Take heart, have faith, for with patience and persistence they can come to be birthed in Divine timing. There is a right time for everything. If you have some big dreams and desires, call them in during the Winter phase or during the New Moon window.

And so, my story of book writing continues.

Feeling more settled in 2018, I felt the calling of my book again. Out she came from the loft, but I realised how much I had changed and evolved. I was a different woman and my Soul had grown.

It was then that magical synchronicity aligned me with the amazing mentor Hannah Gold, who is now an award-winning children's author of *The Last Bear*. I was listening to Facebook Live in another women's group whilst cooking tea. A group I hadn't been in for a very long time suddenly called me. You know when life is bringing you what you need. Hannah was a guest speaker that night and I enjoyed listening to her. She ran the *Soul Writer's Sanctuary*. The next day I contacted her and subsequently joined her membership group. It was here that my writing began to flourish and newfound confidence in my voice was born. I began writing for *Kindred Spirit* magazine and I loved sharing my wisdom of the Sacred Feminine and our connection with Mother Earth. After about 18 months Hannah's new publishing contract took off and she needed to dedicate her time to full-time writing. She handed over the mantle to another amazing mentor, Jo Roberts who really helped me see the value and worth of my writing. She loved *Mother Earth is Calling You* and she helped review and edit my first two drafts of a book that was now growing so huge I was beginning to wonder if I would ever get to finish and birth it.

In January 2022, I decided I needed to take time out to rest and stand back from my business. Surprisingly with this space opening, I felt a strong urge to complete the Winter spiral of my book. By the end of January, I was celebrating. Yes, I had done it and I felt so proud. She was reviewed and edited. But how was I going to get the rest finished alongside my business? I knew I didn't want to put my business on hold but writing alongside wasn't easy with my energy being pulled in different directions.

I was just returning from a walk in Nature, when I received a clear message in my heart, "Publish Winter as your first book. It will be the foundation for the rest of the series to follow." Wow, this felt so aligned, I had heat rising from the Earth through my body in resonance and shivers of excitement down my body. I remember excitedly telling my mentor, Jo, on my next call. She too felt the certainty of this. All I had to do was rewrite Part One to focus just on Winter and finish off with a final chapter... well that's what I thought.

But I realised the Universe had my back. *Mother Earth is Calling You* has its own energy and knows exactly what she needs, to be birthed into the world.

Who was going to be my publisher, who would understand the essence of my book and would honour the process in the way She had been written?

I put out to the Universe, 'Please send me the perfect publishing team who will support me and will be the perfect publisher for *Mother Earth is Calling You*'.

I sat back and waited and got on with serving my business and stitching the pieces of my writing together, pulling out that which was no longer needed and weaving in new threads that came to me as Life flowed through me.

In March 2022, I was part of a Shamanic Dreaming course with Monica Kenton, a Shamanic Dream Teacher, and received this wonderful meditation.

Journal Entry - What is My Book's Next Step?

I found myself in a forest following a pathway that took me to a house. A gatekeeper to the house was standing by the front door. This gatekeeper looked like the Lord of the Forest. He had a falcon sitting on his right shoulder and his outfit was made of dark green cloth. He held a beautiful shining gold key. He offered it to me and with a smile and glee, I opened the house. Feeling excited as I opened, this golden warm air wafted towards me. I found myself in a kitchen with a long wooden table and sitting around the table were several wise women, all smiling, welcoming me and clapping in celebration. I had a sense of feeling at home, comfortable, supported. I could feel there was a bigger purpose for us coming together that was unfolding. Then I saw a gold coin in the centre of the table, twinkling and shining at me.

Then suddenly the scene shifted, and I found myself upstairs – there were gold coins everywhere in abundance. It was amazing. So bright and dazzling. I felt abundance was being offered to me and represented my Soul's worth and wealth. Coming down again, I stepped down a spiral staircase to meet and sit with the women again. Two more gold coins had appeared on the table.

I realised who these women were as I had recently had a call with Nicola Humber, the Founder of Unbound Press. I recognised in this moment, the way *Mother Earth is Calling You* wanted to be birthed is a sacred act of honouring the dark feminine and what better container than a group of loving, supportive women who are to become the midwives for the book you hold in your hands.

Since the dream, I signed up with Unbound Press and continued to edit and weave additional elements to bring everything together.

What is so magical is that I submitted my final manuscript to Nicola on the day of the New Moon in Leo on 28th July 2022. It was not planned in this way, this was how Mother Earth weaved her magic!

Leo is the sign of the courageous Lion and this New Moon is the opening of the Lionsgate that peaks on the eighth day of the eighth month known as the 8:8 Lionsgate Portal each year. The bright light of the Star Sirius and the Leonine Kingdom aligns with the dark of the New Moon, seeding the light in the fertile space of the Dark Moon, our primal feminine. This is a potent time of entering the dark of the New Moon with the light, joy and abundance of the great lion's heart – one that brings the light codes to awaken and assist us to embrace our lion-hearted courage and to rise up from darkness as the glorious sovereign beings we are.

This is especially exciting for me as my sacred home in the Stars is from Sirius and the Lyra star constellation. I am feeling the joy of this synchronistic alignment. Only our souls can weave this kind of magic!

Since the New Moon in Leo, *Mother Earth is Calling You* has travelled with this abundant energy weaving in the codes and light that the Lionsgate Portal has brought through.

Now you have the gift of holding Her in your hands. Open your heart to receive the gold of this time woven through time and space to reach you now.

Acknowledgements

My heartfelt appreciation and thanks go to the many teachers and mentors who have supported me along my path through the ups and downs of the writing journey, and whose wise words each have a unique place in my heart.

Hannah Gold for her inspiration, cheerleading, and trailblazing a path that shows me that miracles and big dreams do become a reality with perseverance and self-belief.

Jo Roberts for her incredible support, being there for me, holding my hand through the early drafts of my book, encouraging and believing in me and the wisdom of *Mother Earth is Calling You: Winter Wisdom* until I was ready to fly and work with my publisher.

Immense gratitude goes to Nicola Humber, for being an inspiring and magical mentor who immediately 'got' me and my book. Who continues to help me go beyond what I thought was possible for myself and my writing – to write beyond my wild edges, to be truly unbound, to trust completely in the journey to birth my book.

All the awesome magical women of Unbound Press, who I am journeying with. They help me feel safe and held and are the cheerleaders and midwives of Winter Wisdom. Special thanks goes to Anna Bromley for her sensitive and skilful copy editing that has made the manuscript polished and shining. Big thanks go to Lynda Mangoro for her beautiful cover design that conveys the magical depths of Winter and all the wizardry she has created to bring everything together inside. To my daughter Louise Hampden and dear friend Caroline Tennant who have provided valuable support and sounding board in bringing Winter Wisdom into beautiful form.

Behind the scenes thanking all my dear friends who believe and support me, who reassure and celebrate with me, including Sally Tyler, Tara Reeves, Caroline Cousins, Tanya Blackiston, Caroline Tennant, Pippa Handley-Cooke, Penny Gundry, Lia Bird and many more that support me in numerous, loving ways.

To all my wonderful clients and women who I have sat in circle with and journeyed with, who have also taught me much. Special thanks go to Kirsty Garland and Tanya Blackiston for sharing their personal stories that have added a richness and depth to Winter Wisdom, that I am truly grateful for.

And closer to home, deep gratitude goes to my family for their ongoing support and loving presence in my life who have helped shape the woman I am today. To our talented creative daughter, Louise Hampden, for creating the beautiful illustrations that echo the essence of the book. I am so proud to have her energy included – a fitting tribute to our mother and father lineage. To our loving son, Ben, who is a wonderful support and sounding board, wise beyond his years, always having a curiosity in my life's work. To my loyal husband, Paul, who stands by me, is my rock and support and my greatest life teacher.

To my mother for bringing me into this world, for caring for me, for encouraging me on my path, for your kindness and for making me laugh. For all the lessons and blessings that have been perfect for my life's journey to come home to myself, including the journey with my dear sisters. To my loving father, now in heaven, but whose love and strength is with me always. *Mother Earth is Calling You* is a testament to our lineage.

To all my mentors, coaches and teachers who have supported me on life's magical journey, for the incredible growth, their love and support and the wisdom gained, that has helped me journey deeper to embrace my authentic self, including: Diana Summer for my first initiation on the journey to discover the Goddess within me. Aehlah Brandon, for always being there when I most needed, for her healing, incredible shamanic journeys that helped me embrace my shadows and find my hidden treasures. Kalindi Jordan, who helped me reignite my sexual life force and the joy of reconnecting with my sacred womb that propelled me on a journey to support other women to do the same. To Sophia Schorr-Kon for her gentle holding that has enabled much beautiful transformation in my life. Monica Kenton for her joyful inspiration and shamanic teachings and visions. Sue Coulson for facilitating amazing cosmic journeys for planetary healing, that have helped me expand to reconnect with my multi-dimensional self and connect with my loving Star brothers and sisters.

To the Councils of Light, my spiritual team in the unseen realms. Thank you for standing by me, loving me unconditionally and for your constant whispers, wisdom and guidance that has supported me throughout my life. Helping me to trust in my magnificence and perfect Divine timing.

To beloved Mother Earth, my rock and foundation and source of wisdom and abundant beauty. To the magical Universe, I thank you for the miracle of life that always leaves me in awe.

Finally, to all my dear readers. Thank you for answering the call, to listening to your inner wisdom and rising up in your magnificence.

Journalling Tips

Journalling is:

- An active way of committing to your journey.
- A space where you can meet and connect with your authentic Self.
- A way to unload your mind and unravel jumbled thoughts.
- A new perspective and pathway through a troubling situation.
- Renewed inspiration and a way to ground your ideas.
- Expressing difficult emotions and grief.
- Letting go of frustrations and confusion.
- Gaining clarity for your goals and dreams to make them concrete.
- Expressing gratitude for the blessings in your life.

If you are not familiar with journalling and have some resistance, you are not alone. Initially turning up to a blank piece of paper can be daunting. We have been taught to identify a purpose and to expect a specific result. Journalling offers the opposite, a way to let go of expectations and allow ourselves to write freely whatever comes into our minds.

In Julia Cameron's book, The Artist's Way, she shares a simple yet powerful exercise that is called 'Morning Pages' which has helped hundreds of people to unlock writer's block.

Julia suggests that first thing in the morning, before you start your day, to take some paper and write whatever comes into your mind. She identifies this as a way to unload and unravel thoughts and confusion. She suggests timing yourself, say starting initially with 10 minutes. During this time allowing your pen to flow unhindered.

Of course, you could do it anytime of the day when you feel you have a cluttered mind and cannot think clearly.

Here is a way to start your journalling.

1. First take a blank piece of paper and pen.

2. Time yourself say for 10 minutes or longer if you are more experienced.

3. Start writing the first thing that comes into your mind. Suspend all judgement and expectation. You can't get it wrong, it just is. If you hear, 'I don't know what to write?' Write just that and then the next thing and so on.

Often it is a matter of just turning up to a blank page and allowing the first words to be written. They may not make sense or mean anything initially but as you write and get the thoughts out of the way, people often describe they let go of frustrations and a peace comes over them as a new stream of consciousness begins to flow.

If your writing does not happen straight away, just enjoy the moment of writing what you can and in time you may notice a difference in your outlook and the way you perceive a situation. This is a time to recognise how far you have come. Perhaps the old patterns and thoughts that occupied your mind will no longer take centre stage.

The first thing is to treat yourself to a new journal, one that will inspire you to keep coming back to the page to connect with yourself.

Resources and Further Reading

Moonology by Yasmin Boland

Wisdom of the Elements by Margie McArthur

Earth Wisdom by Glennie Kindred

The Tree Ogham by Glennie Kindred

The Spirit of Trees by Fred Hageneder

Unbound by Nicola Humber

Wild Power by Alexandra Pope and Sjanie Hugo Wurlitzer

Wise Power: Discover the Liberating Power of Menopause to Awaken Authority, Purpose and Belonging by Alexandra Pope and Sjanie Hugo Wurlitzer

Light is the New Black Rebecca Campbell

Love Your Lady Landscape by Lisa Lister

Womb Wisdom Padma and Anaiya Aon Prakasha

The Wisdom of the Menopause by Christiane Northrup, MD

Resources and Links

Monica Kenton, Active Dream Teacher and Spiritual Advisor: https://www.monicakenton.com/

The Four Winds Society: https://thefourwinds.com

Kindred Spirit Magazine link here: https://kindredspirit.co.uk/

Women's Circles

The Red Tent: https://redtentdirectory.com/

Sources for Cacao Plant Medicine

Oh My Goddess Ceremonial Cacao only shipped within UK:

https://www.ohmygoddess.uk/#/

Soundscapes on Spotify and Youtube

Wise Woman Song – 'Woman Deep Down in the Woods' by Elaine Cullinane:

https://spoti.fi/3gh0NNU

Steffy Oren Bach's *Grandmother Song*:

https://spoti.fi/3eKq1Uk

Cacao Spirit Song by Lovechock on Youtube

Guided Meditations and Soundscapes

www.sonrayagrace.com/winter-book-resources

www.sonrayagrace.com/meditations-to-buy-and-keep/

Youtube: Sonraya Grace

About the Author

Sonraya is a Rebirth Doula, Earth Wisdom Keeper, Soulful Intuitive Healer, and Spiritual Alchemist with over 25 years' experience in the healing arts. She lives close to the sea in Dorset, UK with her husband and their cat, Mysty. They have two grown up children and love to spend quality time with family and loved ones. Sonraya's greatest joy is to walk by the sea and be in Nature which offer a constant source of nourishment and inspiration.

Sonraya is passionate about supporting women to activate and reclaim their Sacred Feminine power and wisdom, in sacred union with their Sacred Masculine. She empowers them to align with their truth, to awaken the power of their voice so they can fully express their wild, authentic nature. She is dedicated to sharing her wisdom and serving her community, supporting the global shift towards unity consciousness.

Sonraya holds sacred space for transformation so that your true magic can unfurl.

She offers:

Online Women's Circles and Events

In person retreat days and weekends

One to one session both online and in person in Dorset.

Ancestral healing, sacred womb healing and rite of passage, sacred ceremony, and rituals in honour of the Earth and the Sacred Feminine.

Shamanic Soul Journey and Women's Shamanic Drum Circles

Sound Healing with Voice.

Stay Connected:

For full details please visit her website: www.sonrayagrace.com

Guided Meditations: www.sonrayagrace.com/winter-book-resources

Facebook: www.facebook.com/SonrayaGrace

Instagram: www.instagram.com/sarahsonraya/

Printed in Great Britain
by Amazon

14045759R00169